COMPOST GARDENING

COMPOST GARDENING

W. E. SHEWELL-COOPER
MBE, NDH, CDH, FLS, FRSL, DLitt

DAVID & CHARLES
NEWTON ABBOT LONDON VANCOUVER

0 7153 6773 0

This is the second edition, revised in content and format, of the book first published in 1972

Second impression 1976

Printed in Great Britain
by Ebenezer Baylis & Son Ltd Worcester
for David & Charles (Publishers) Limited
Brunel House Newton Abbot Devon

Published in Canada
by Douglas David & Charles Limited
1875 Welch Street North Vancouver BC

CONTENTS

ILLUSTRATIONS

Drawings

Illustrations not otherwise acknowledged are from the author's collection.

PREFACE

Giving birth to a new book is tremendously exciting, and particularly so in the case of *Compost Gardening*, which I so gladly dedicate to the President of the Good Gardeners' Association. Those who are dedicated to gardening with the minimum of work plus the maximum results, will I think like the book. It describes gardening without chemical fertilisers or harmful sprays explaining how to grow flowers with magnificent colours and scents, vegetables with the good old-fashioned flavour and food value, and fruit delicious to eat.

The Arkley Manor Gardens, near Barnet, Hertfordshire, have become famous among people who garden organically. In the twelve years that they have been established, no digging or forking have been done, and the only hoeing has been in the vegetable garden, four or five times a year. The garden is maintained in accordance with the advice in this book, and the results are there for all to see. The rose beds, for instance, which were mulched with powdery compost or with peat humus ten years or so ago and have never had to be hoed, are a real testimony to the value of this no-digging, no-hoeing system.

It must be said, of course, that I live and garden in a temperate climate. In this book I refer to many plants which grow in this climate but may not grow in yours. You on the other hand may be able to grow plants which I grow only under special conditions. Compost gardening works no matter what types of plant you grow. It is regrettable that I cannot describe every section of every country in detail but the size of this book dictates that I remain as it were a general adviser. Just remember regardless of where you live compost gardening will produce larger, healthier and more productive plants, with less work for you. If you wish more specific information about the plants in your locality talk to other organic gardeners around you and consult with your local nurseries and greenhouses. As a reader of this book, I hope that you too will join The Good Gardeners' Association, so that you may receive the regular monthly bulletins and be able to have your soil analysed free. In America you also can receive valuable advice from the Dept of Agriculture Extension Service located in your county town or state capital—but remember that only a few of the officers in the Service are compost-minded, so that you may be advised to use chemical fertilisers, which of course is not 'compost gardening'.

I wish to thank my son, C. R. G. Shewell-Cooper, CDH, for his interest and help in preparing this book, and Mrs Sue Enfield for typing the script so patiently.

W. E. SHEWELL-COOPER, 1972

The Good Gardeners' Association
Arkley Manor
Near Barnet
Hertfordshire

1

THE BASIC APPROACH

THOUSANDS of people today realise that chemicals have harmed both the soil and the plants grown in it. It is quite normal to hear complaints about the tastelessness of food, the scentlessness of flowers and the 'mealiness' of apples and pears. Wholefood shops or 'health stores' flourish, and one of the biggest wholesalers in London's Covent Garden, T. J. Poupart, has a compost-grown food department.

People want to know what to do to have better gardens with plants freer from pests and diseases, without working themselves to death or incurring heavy expense. This book gives an answer; for twenty years now the author has run a famous 8-acre garden without any chemical fertiliser, and without doing any digging, hoeing or forking. The garden is free from weeds and is genuinely beautiful, prolific and profitable.

What is 'compost gardening' and how does it work? Basically it is simply a matter of giving priority to ensuring that the supply of usable food to the plants is maintained. This is done by regularly adding compost and other organic material to the surface of the soil.

THE IMPORTANCE OF HUMUS

Humus must be considered the 'life blood of the living earth', vital to healthy plant growth. A man with no blood is dead—and soil with no humus is equally dead and useless. The desert that has of recent years emerged in North America's Middle West, covering millions of acres, is the result of wheat being grown and its straw burnt for some fifty years, only artificial fertilisers being added, so that the soil was gradually robbed of its humus content; thus the soil 'died'. It must be remembered that there are market gardens in China that have been cultivated intensively and continuously for forty centuries—and the soil is still in perfect condition today. The Chinese peasants have realised the importance of passing back into the soil what has been taken out, so that the soil bacteria can produce the necessary humus. We gardeners have to realise that 'everything that has lived can live again in a plant'. Thus the beginning of the humus story is found in the compost heap.

What is this humus? Is it decayed and decaying organic matter? People often take me to see a heap of rotted leaves and say 'Look at that nice humus', but rotted leaves are not humus. I have been shown half-rotted sawdust and told that it is humus. Mushroom growers sometimes refer to the 'terreau' in which the mushrooms are grown as humus, which of course it is not. Humus is a composite entity, possessing chemical, biological and physical properties which make it distinct from all other natural bodies. It is in fact a complex residue of partially oxidised animal and vegetable matter, together with substances synthesised by beneficial fungi and bacteria. It has a most valuable coagulating effect on sandy soil and an opening-up effect on heavy clay soil, improving their respective textures so that they will retain water—vital in periods of drought—without losing their crumbly quality and becoming waterlogged.

Some may be surprised that humus is so complex in character—but it must be remembered that one of its functions is to be a food to other micro-organisms and creatures. During the formation of humus all sorts of chemical changes take place, for the organisms in the earth work on the dead plant and animal tissue present, breaking them down into simpler substances, the simple chemicals on which plants can feed. Humus must be continually replenished if the soil is to be kept in the right healthy condition, for it steadily disappears as the bacteria work on, and the more intensively the soil is cultivated the faster this process becomes.

Arkley Manor (*author*)

In a handful of ordinary garden soil there may be—should be—millions of living organisms. The various types of bacteria do different jobs; some will attack the cellulose in any dead plant-roots present; some are really the scavengers of the soil. Some concentrate on the proteins and carbohydrates, and others on the nitrogenous matter. Roughly speaking, one microbe does a job and when this job is finished another comes along with all his friends and deals with the breaking-down problem in the particular conditions created by the first. In fact sometimes the first set of microbes are actually absorbed by the second set. What the bacteria are doing, of course, is setting about the preparation of food for the generations that are to come.

Working close to the bacteria is the humble earthworm. He is very important to us, but few seem to give him his rightful place! The earthworm is naked and blind and has no teeth or claws, in fact no weapons of defence or offence. He has no mind to be afraid and no feet to run away—yet, as Charles Darwin wrote, 'It may be doubted whether there are many animals which have played so important a part in the history of the world as have these lowly organised creatures.' The earthworm has the power continually to renew and maintain the valuable film of the top soil. Bits of all the waste products of life go through his body, the dead leaves, the bird and animal manure, the dead bodies of insects, birds, mice, rats and so on. Animal and vegetable life in all its forms, from man down to microbe, whatever has lived and died, is the food of the earthworm.

Travelling all over the world, it has been interesting to note the type of earthworms. Darwin said they were particularly big in the Sudan—I have found enormous ones in Australia, so large and strong, in fact, that they can penetrate quite hard 'pans' of soil. There is no such thing as soil that has no earthworm 'capsules' (eggs), except perhaps in the middle of the Sahara. I have been shown some soils in Canada, Bermuda, Malta, Mauritius and Tasmania, for instance, which were supposed to be worm-free, but the moment deep cultivations were stopped, the moment compost was made and put on top of the ground, the moment that pure chemical fertilisers were not used, the capsules hatched out and the worms started to populate the soil.

When one learns that one worm can produce 600 wormlings in a year and when one realises that a wormling only 90 days old can reproduce—then the possibility of increasing the worm population as if by magic becomes clear. The numbers of worms, are, of course, influenced by soil environment. The distribution of the earthworm population is never constant. The numbers change in accordance with the supply of organic matter, the acidity of the soil—the moisture content and the temperature and texture.

These worms not only tunnel, to a depth of 3ft or more, and produce a perfect soil structure, but they swallow portions of soil and chew these up in their calciferous gland. When they regurgitate the chewed-up soil they produce a worm cast (as it is called) and this contains five times more nitrogen, seven times more phosphate, and eleven times more potash than the soil which was swallowed originally. Thus the worms add plant foods to the soil and so they help to keep the earth fertile. They do all the digging, as it were, and they see to it that they take the compost where it is needed. I have known the worms to go down to 5 and 6ft in very frosty weather and when the soil makes this necessary.

Humus may be thought of as the bridge between life and death in the soil. It is, as it were, the transition stage between one form of life and another. It is a colloid, looking like a kind of brownish-black jelly. Its presence makes all the difference to a gardener's success. Eat a delicious cake and you do not see the eggs in it, but it is those fresh eggs that have made all the difference. Humus is like that. Have plenty present, and the soil is in good health. It is the jelly-like substance that prevents soil from being mere dust. (That is why it seems a pity that the translators of the Authorised Version of the Bible gave the Hebrew word 'aphar', in Genesis iii, 19, as 'dust'; its real meaning, as leading Hebrew scholars have accepted, is undoubtedly humus!)

Humus, then, is the life of the soil, the organic colloid that causes the soil to live. It is made from substances that were once alive, and it can help to promote life. It is able to store plant foods and prevent them from being leached out of the soil. It gives the ideal protection against heat and cold, drought and waterlogging. The soil is not only an anchorage for the roots of the plants, and a vast storehouse of plant foods; it is a large manufacturing centre, with millions of living organisms working morning, noon and night. Yet there can be no permanently perfect soil. Every piece of work done in the garden helps to break down humus and every crop grown reduces the organic content of the soil: so replacement of the humus must be a gardener's priority. A vigorous, living, breathing soil is what is required, a soil from which the capital—the humus—is never removed. Where there is no capital, there is of course no dividend.

How compost maintains the humus in the soil

The compost gardener therefore covers the surface of the soil with material on which the bacteria can work—with compost, made from all the garden and household rubbish of an organic nature, as described in Chapter 2. If you cannot, or have not, made compost, use peat humus. As the compost or peat is spread on the top, there is no need to do any digging. Because there is no digging, there is less breakdown of the humus in the earth. In the vegetable garden, where seeds are to be sown, the compost may be lightly forked or raked in: I use a rotary cultivator for this purpose only, cultivating the soil to a depth of 1in.

In the rose garden, shrub or herbaceous borders, heather gardens, iris beds, primula garden, hemerocallis garden, red-hot-poker garden and so on, whatever you may have, the compost is put all over the soil after planting, 1in deep, and is never disturbed.

Thus all the annual weeds are suppressed. In nearly all soils there are millions of weed seeds in the top few inches. Every time the gardener hoes he brings up hundreds of seeds which germinate when they find themselves near the surface. If you never hoe, they never reach the top, and those already on the surface of the soil ready to grow are prevented from doing so by the compost covering. This incidentally makes the whole garden look more attractive. Just think of it with no annual weeds like crab grass, purslane, pigweed, chickweed, shepherd's purse, groundsel, nettles, etc—the soil looking warm, brown, well-cared for. The worms will enjoy the surface mulch of organic matter and will multiply and work, pulling in what they need. They much dislike a dry soil, in which their tunnels break up. Leave the soil alone, however, and they will do their job, tunnelling down 3ft and more, providing channels down which the air, moisture and plant foods can go. The worms therefore do all the digging for the gardener, and he has none to do for himself. There are gardens all over the world today that are never dug, and countless men and women who cannot tackle heavy digging are thus enabled to enjoy growing the plants they choose.

Compost should be rich in natural vitamins, which of course come from the leaves and stems that were thrown on the heap, as discussed in the next chapter. It contains anti-biotica and enzymes. Thus the spreading of the powdery compost on top of the ground does far more than our grandparents' favourite farmyard manure would do; it not only feeds, it provides natural protection from disease for the plants.

Peat humus may be described as nature's compost. The grasses, sedge and rushes were composted by the activation of the manure from birds and wild animals thousands of years ago forming peat which is lifted and sold as peat humus. It can be used all over the garden as an alternative to compost by those starting a new garden who will not have had a chance to make their own compost, or by those who cannot make enough from their household and garden refuse. Peat humus should not be confused with the much more common peat moss. Peat moss is nothing more than dry fibres of moss. The fibres have not decomposed or composted so therefore cannot add nourishment to the soil. In fact the process of decomposing requires nutriments which will be taken to the detriment of your plants. Peat humus can be expensive and since it is lifted in limited quantities in some areas, it can be hard to find. If you live near an area where it is available you might be able to buy a large quantity at considerable savings especially if you can combine your order with some neighbours. Another alternative is to buy one of the commercially prepared organic composts which are on the market. These organic substitutes will suffice for a small town garden or will help you get started while you wait for your own compost to mature.

THE USE OF CHEMICAL FERTILISERS

Some people have assumed that the minerals the chemical fertilisers contain are taken up and used by the plants. This, in fact is not true, as research has proved. Plants in soil fed with compost only take up more minerals than plants in gardens fed with chemical fertilisers. The analysis of the soil, as well as the analysis made of all the crops grown in the compost-only plot as well as those grown on the chemical fertilisers-fed plot, has shown that the addition of fertilisers is not necessarily connected with fertility. In fact that word has now lost its original

The strip herb garden at the author's Arkley Manor gardens; grown without any digging, forking or hoeing

meaning. M. E. Brown, of the Rothamsted Experimental Station, has pointed out that the 'zone' of soil subject to the roots of a plant supports far greater microbial activity than other areas in the soil. Plant growth may therefore be increased if the organisms make available to the roots foods that are normally in an unavailable form. This they will do, if there are enough of them. It is possible, for instance, for the bacteria to make available what are known as *unavailable* phosphates. An agricultural chemist may analyse a soil and find that the phosphate content is low. He may therefore mistakenly advise the use of chemical phosphates at so much per square yard—when in fact the organisms in the earth could produce naturally all the phosphates needed, at no expense to the garden owner.

Compost not only feeds the soil but, because the bacteria it encourages are able to produce from it lots and lots of humus, helps hold the moisture in it. This is tremendously important when you remember that the weight of some vegetables consists of more than 90 per cent water. It is said that in Europe nature normally provides 3,000 tons of water to the acre each year. But in soil insufficiently full of humus, 49 per cent of this rainfall is lost through evaporation and 20 per cent can easily flow out and away. On the other hand when there is sufficient compost in the earth, it can easily hold 69 per cent of the rainfall that comes down; in fact experiments have shown that 180lb of water can easily be absorbed by 100lb of compost. This is why composted land emerges so well in and after a drought.

I said earlier that it is important that compost should not be buried deeply in the soil, because when this is done the soil itself compresses the compost, reducing its water-holding capacity. A heavy rainfall under those compressed conditions saturates the soil quickly, silts up the channels and air passages made by the worms, and undoubtedly stifles, as a result, the natural aeration and the drainage. Thus by burying too deep you ruin the very object for which the soil is dug. When you put the compost on top of the soil, or rotovate it into the top 2in, the earth remains undisturbed so that the bacteria are able to continue to work. The compost itself, because it is not compressed, will absorb the rainwater to its fullest capacity. Any surplus water there may be will undoubtedly wash small particles of the compost into the upper layer of soil and leave free the air passages and channels made by the worms, for aeration and rain.

Those who are keen on chemical fertilisers have to agree with me that they cannot produce 1oz of humus to give to the soil. *Chemicals in fact feed the plant direct, and this is not, nor ever can be, the natural—or most efficient—system.* The natural cycle is for you to feed the soil and the soil in its turn to feed the plant.

An interesting series of experiments illustrated this point. It was discovered that to get a nice early lettuce with a really firm crisp heart, the important thing was to ensure that in the baby seedlings stage the leaves were rich in potash—a case of look after the baby, and you will have a wonderful adult. So some plants were grown in soil given 5cwt of sulphate of potash per acre, other plants in soil given 10cwt of sulphate of potash per acre, and yet a third group in soil given 15cwt per acre. Yet those little plants would not take in any extra potash; they would only be persuaded to do so when the ground was fed with an organic manure. Then, and only then did the little plants take up the extra potash they needed, with excellent results.

There are knowledgeable scientists who will point out that potash is an element, and that therefore it makes no difference whether you give it in an organic form or a purely chemical form. The fact remains, however, that the plants do seem to know the difference; as I have said, undoubtedly we farmers and gardeners must learn to feed the soil, and then let the millions of living organisms in the earth feed the plant. There is no magic in composting; it is not a miracle worker; it is merely the perfect food for the miracle workers (ie the flora and fauna of the soil), and it is these that produce the fantastically successful results I have seen again and again.

There is much careless talk about chemical fertilisers and, of course, tremendous vested interests are behind the publicity stressing the 'need' for them. Look at the pages of any popular gardening magazine and you will be offered fertiliser this and fertiliser that. Yet a famous soil chemist, Dr R. F. Milton, has been able to show at the Haughley Research Station in Suffolk that the addition of inorganic salts (in the shape of fertilisers) represses the bacterial activity and such repression is of course contrary to the classic natural system of fertility. Further, Dr Milton has been able to show that the use of chemical fertilisers, instead of encouraging the seasonal increase in available plant nutrients, actually reduces the natural production. Left alone, the soil bacteria work hard and raise the plant-food content of the soil, so that more is available in the summer, when needed, than in the winter.

It is the physical condition of the soil that is so important. When the denizens of the soil are really 'happy' and can work in an unrestricted manner, on plenty of organic material, such as compost supplies, they undoubtedly produce the right results. It is when there are constant cultivations with the idea of controlling weeds that the soil is depleted of organic matter. The keen organic gardener therefore will not hoe continually but will apply the powdery compost, the peat humus, or similar organic matter, on top of the ground as a mulch, an inch or so deep. He will not be troubled with annual weeds.

Disease and humus

It has been suggested that when organic matter is used regularly in your soil, so that the humus content is really high, the food produced by it can actually immunise the human body from certain ills; I would never dare to go as far as that. I prefer to put it another way, that when the ground is continually fed with chemical manure the food produced on the land is lacking in 'something' and this lack may contribute to human lack of resistance to many modern human disorders.

The excellent health of the Hunza tribe in the North West Frontier area of India cannot be put down to the locality in which they live, for the Ishkominas also live under apparently the same conditions as their neighbours, are poor, under-sized and under-nourished creatures. Ishkominas burn their refuse and animal manure, while the Hunzas in their manuring use everything they can return to the soil. They collect all the vegetable refuse which will not serve as food to man or beast, and they mix it with dung; they even use the human sewage after they have kept it for six months. They also eat their food fresher on the whole than we do in the Western world, though like us they are also bread-eaters. They, however, prefer to eat their bread made with the whole content of the grain with its vital germ and its protective skin, while most people today eat white bread, for which the husk of the grain is removed during the process of milling. In Sir Robert McCarrison's Mallan lecture on 'Faulty Food in Relation to Gastro-Intestinal Disorder', he states, 'During my period of association with the Hunza people I never saw a case of dyspepsia, of gastric or duodenal ulcer, of appendicitis or cancer. The point about the Hunzas who live in the northern part of Kashmir is that their agriculture is perfect. They use organic manure only; they carry out fully the law of return, and they do not use artificial fertilisers or poison sprays.'

2

MAKING AND APPLYING COMPOST

IN the previous chapter, the importance of humus has been stressed. Humus is made in the soil itself by millions of living organisms, and the gardener cannot add it—he must add organic matter, which the worms will pull into the ground or which he will lightly fork in, and this will be converted gradually by the bacteria, the 'flora and fauna', into usable food for the plants.

It helps the soil organisms greatly if much of the work of this conversion is done in the compost heap. This heap can be likened in a way to the bee, which digests the nectar into the sugary food much beloved by children, before depositing it in the comb; thus honey can be called pre-digested food. Compost can be considered as partially digested vegetable waste which is well on the way to being made into humus. When fresh green matter is added to the soil, as it is when people apply lawn mowings as a top dressing, the worms of course pull some of it into the ground, in the same way as they draw into the soil any other organic matter. The soil bacteria have then to work on this fresh material, but to do so they have to rob the ground of nitrogen, and the plants in consequence suffer. This problem with 'green manuring', as it is called, is known by gardeners as denitrification.

It is, therefore, tremendously necessary to know how to make good compost. Very few people in fact do this. It's perhaps even more important for the town dweller than the country dweller, for the soil of the town garden is invariably in poor condition. And a rubbish heap in the corner of the garden is definitely *not* a compost heap. On a rubbish heap, you just chuck any vegetable waste you want to get rid of; a compost heap is treated in a very serious manner.

First of all, no bonfires, please! Most men love making bonfires but they burn large quantities of organic matter which should go on the compost heap, and rob the ground of valuable humus and plant foods. Soil which is crying out for organic matter is merely given a few ashes! (Furthermore, the smoke from a bonfire may be even more injurious to lungs than tobacco smoke.) Only burn on a bonfire any really dead wood which cannot possibly rot down on the compost heap. It will burn quickly, producing hardly any smoke, and further, the wood ash that results is rich in potash and may go on to the compost heap to improve it. It can be applied also along rows of raspberries, strawberries, gooseberries and tomatoes, at the rate of ½lb to the yard run; these fruits like 'extra' potash when available.

WHAT CAN BE COMPOSTED?

The statement that 'everything that has lived can live again in another plant' must be repeated, and it must be understood. There are far too many self-elected experts who state categorically that you must not put rhubarb leaves, laurel leaves, privet leaves and even potash haulm on to the compost heap. Others will say that no seedling weeds or diseased plants, or even plants that have been attacked by insect pests, should go there. These experts are wrong—very wrong. If a compost heap is made properly, the great heat engendered in the heap, perhaps reaching 180° F, will be enough to kill all the weed seeds, and all the diseases and pests as well. There is no living plant that will not rot down perfectly on a compost heap and produce the desired result. Therefore, an organic gardener will collect from his home, as well as from the garden, everything that has lived, and will put it systematically on to his compost heap, layer by layer, and let it rot down.

The author in one of his compost bins

The kind of products that will be used are tea leaves, coffee grounds, banana or orange skins, the fluff from the vacuum cleaner, old woollen stockings, old silk stockings (but never nylon stockings, for these of course have never lived), eggshells, dead flowers, potato and apple peelings, the outsides of cauliflowers, the pods of peas, and all the newspaper once it has been torn up and soaked in water. Incidentally, newspapers may be laid flat, sheet by sheet, in between layers of lawn mowings, and will help to rot them down properly.

From the garden, you can use the lawn mowings, the leaves from all the trees, the tops of the carrots and beetroots, the tops of the artichokes, the leaves of the celery, the cut-down herbaceous plants, weeds of all kinds, the old bedding plants, the fresh hedge clippings. All these will be added as they become available, and as the heap rises the top of each layer should be kept flat and level.

MAKING THE HEAP

It is best to make the heap in a wooden bin, and the planks that make its three sides should have 1in spaces in between them to let the air into the heap—for the bacteria that convert the waste into compost need air to breathe if they are to work well. Wood is better than galvanised iron or concrete because it's warmer. For a big garden, the bin can be say 8ft by 8ft; for a garden of around half an acre, say 6ft by 6ft; for a small garden, under about a quarter-acre, 4ft by 4ft. (At Arkley, where I have 8 acres, the bins are 10ft square, and there are five of them in all.) The collected compost material can be wheeled into position from the open end. Whatever the size, it is convenient to have the bin about 6 or 7ft high. Every time more waste is put on the heap, it rises slightly, but every time it *must* be kept level: if this is neglected, then the heap will not heat up evenly.

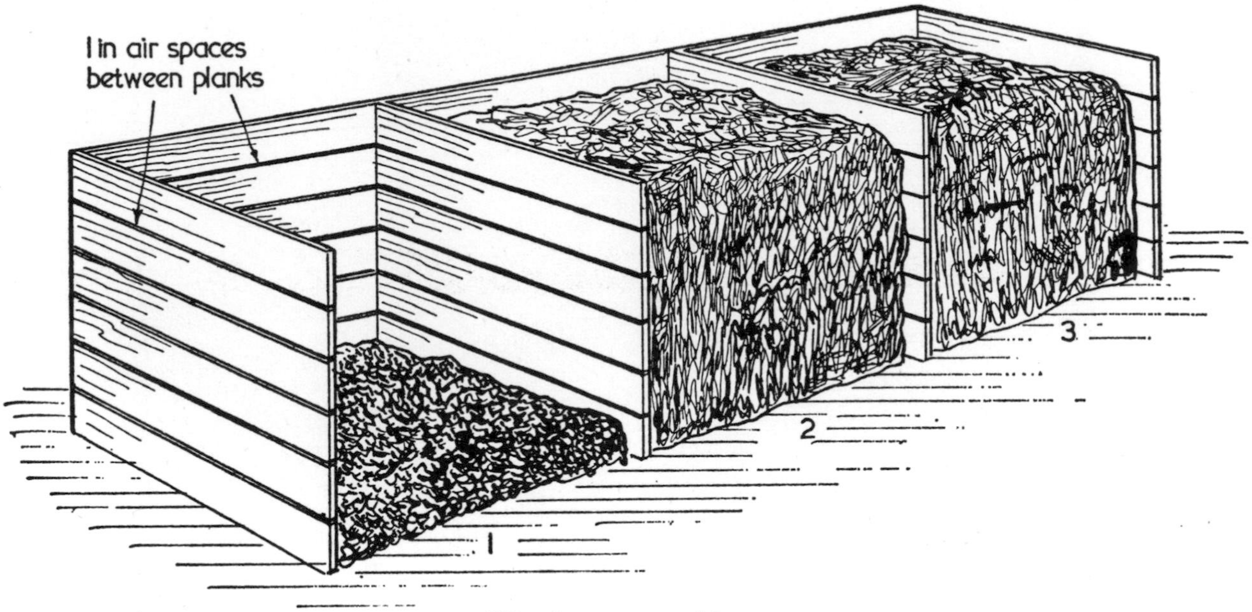

Wooden compost bins

The moment there is a 6in depth of level vegetable waste, the gardener must apply what is called an activator, a food for the bacteria that are going to work on the vegetable matter, and start to break it down. The activator should itself be something that has lived, and it is possible to use poultry manure, pigeon manure, rabbit manure or in fact any other animal manure, but most people prefer to buy fish, blood or seaweed manure which give excellent results. For every 6in thickness of vegetable waste collected, the fish manure, or its equivalent, is applied at 3oz to the square yard.

A true compost heap, therefore, rises layer by layer like the proverbial sponge cake, the jam being the fish manure or what have you. There is a 6in layer of vegetable waste which has been raked and trodden level, then the sprinkling of fish manure; another 6in layer of vegetable waste, and then another sprinkling of fish manure; and so on, right up to the top of the heap. When the 7ft height is reached, it is convenient to cover the top of the heap with a layer of soil 1in deep or with thick blankets, the idea being to keep in the heat and to keep out excess wet. The heap is now left for six months, so that the bacteria can get to work, and so that the worms can do their job as well.

It's important, incidentally, to have the bottom of the heap on the soil and not to make a concrete base, as some people do. The idea is to give the worms an opportunity of tunnelling their way up from the soil into the heap above. Actually, when the heap gets very hot, they burrow their way down again and wait patiently below ground for the heap to cool down once

Two handfuls of powdery home-made compost

more, then wriggling up again. In bigger gardens it is useful to be able to have more than one compost heap, so that while one lot of compost is rotting down and ripening, the second can be in the process of being made; even better, of course, to have three bins, one being filled, one ripening, and a third ready to use.

HOW TO USE COMPOST

Compost making may not sound an important or glamorous activity, but it really is the beginning of all good organic gardening. In the vegetable garden where it is desired to sow seeds, the compost can be forked into the ground 2in or so deep and no more, at the rate of 5 good bucketsful to the square yard. There is no need to do any deep digging. Similarly, in places where flower seeds are to be sown the compost can be lightly forked in first. Everywhere else in the garden, however, the well-rotted browny-black powdery compost is put on to the surface of the ground to act as a top dressing, or a mulch, as gardeners call it. It can be applied at any time of the year, about 1in deep, and as has already been said, must go all over the surface of the soil and not just in a ring around the trees or plants.

Thus the 1in layer of compost goes all over the ground in the case of the shrub borders, the herbaceous border, the soft-fruit plot, the cut-flower section, the michaelmas-daisy bed, the iris bed, and of course the rose beds. The whole idea of this top dressing is to make it quite unnecessary to do any forking or hoeing.

Do not ever let people say that compost is just a good substitute for dung: for creating humus, and for producing anti-biotics, for providing vitamins, and for feeding plants it is much better than dung. If you haven't the opportunity of making compost, buy peat humus instead. This again is not a substitute for dung; it is better than dung and is free from weeds, diseases and pests as well. Use it, for instance, 1in deep on all the rose beds. This makes hoeing quite unnecessary. It may be applied any time, but preferably for the first time in the spring. Once the 1in layer has been spread, it is only necessary to top up with another ¼in of compost once a year, probably for one to four years as described in the next chapter, so as to make up the quantity that has been pulled into the soil by worms. The same system can be used with flowering shrub borders, heather gardens, and herbaceous borders. This principle is right, ie the application from above—the building-up in fact, of the top layers of soil, ensuring they are rich in humus. It helps greatly if, in addition, an organic fertiliser like fish manure can be used at 3 or 4oz to the square yard.

It is always a good thing to grow soft fruits in a plot on their own, and when this is done one can ensure the heaviest yields of delicious berries really rich in the right flavour if again the whole of the surface of the soil is covered with compost. The compost must be applied literally all over the earth occupied by the fruit: so many people have misunderstood the instructions in the past, and have only used it along the rows themselves. No cultivations have to be done at all for the years that follow, and any plant foods that are needed can be applied over the compost and allowed to trickle through naturally as the rain washes them down. With soft fruits, too, incidentally, it pays to use a fish fertiliser in addition, at 3oz to the square yard, say in April and again in late August.

The placing of the organic matter on the surface of the soil gives tremendous encouragement to the worms. They get busy pulling the surface material into the soil and thus they are working up and down continuously, maybe to a depth of 6ft, providing the natural, almost vertical, channels down which the moisture and air can percolate. This is of course particularly useful in heavy soils.

GIVING A FILLIP

In addition to the regular use of compost or peat humus on the soil, it is possible to give plants and extra fillip by the use of an organic fertiliser—like fish manure. There is a type of fish manure which is rich in potash, and this can be given to roses, sweet peas, dessert apples, gooseberries, raspberries, strawberries and tomatoes which particularly like potash. The other usual fish manure contains a normal quantity of potash and may be used for all other plants at the rate of about 3oz to the square yard. There are of course other organic fertilisers, such as meat and bone meal or hoof and horn meal, that can be applied if preferred. There are also proprietary organic plant foods, some made from dung, and some from liquid seaweed. These are used in accordance with the instructions on the containers.

Other organic fertilisers that may be used will be mentioned from time to time, such as steamed bone flour and dried blood; the former to give added phosphates which are so useful for encouraging root growth, the latter to encourage more leaf growth, and therefore often used on brussels sprouts and cabbages.

TEN ESSENTIAL POINTS IN COMPOSTING

1 Have a wooden bin always— square.
2 Keep the 6in layers of waste absolutely level.
3 Apply the organic activator at 3oz to the square yard.
4 The base to the compost bin must be the soil.
5 Allow 1in spaces in between the planks that form the three sides of the bin.
6 Put flat sheets of newspapers in between 2in layers of lawn mowings to prevent them going soggy.
7 Cover the top of the heap with old army blankets, or a 1in thickness of soil.
8 If the material and the weather is very dry, water the heap well.
9 Leave the heap to ripen for six months or in the winter eight months.
10 The heap must heat up to 180° F, or 60° C, and so kill all the diseases, pests and weed seeds. The resultant material should be a dark brown powder. This is compost.

3

LOOKING AFTER THE COMPOST GARDEN

IF the properly composted vegetable matter is put on top of the soil as a thickish brown 'powder', or a 1in layer of peat humus is used, the soil is not disturbed, so no weed seeds are brought to the surface and the annual weeds do not appear. The only weeds that can grow are those springing from odd seeds dropped by birds or blown by wind on the top of the compost. It's a simple matter to tweak these little weeds out with the thumb and forefinger, and they are few enough.

SOIL CULTIVATION

Therefore, in the greater part of the garden, mechanical cultivations are not required. There is no need to hoe in the flower borders, the shrub borders, the herbaceous borders, the soft-fruit plot and the rose beds. The only place where regular mechanical cultivations are needed is the vegetable garden. There the gardener can use a light rotary cultivator with the idea of disturbing the top 2in or so of soil, in order to provide what is called a fine tilth, in which he can easily sow the seeds. During the process of rototilling the compost or peat humus can be incorporated, while if a fish manure is to be used in addition to the compost it can be applied before rototilling also.

The two drawbacks to a mechanical cultivator are firstly that it is rather noisy, and secondly that it is somewhat expensive and it isn't everyone who wants to buy a rotary cultivator in order to save forking. There's no doubt, however, that a much finer tilth is produced by a cultivator than by normal forking, even if this is only done to a depth of 2 or 3in. You can use a garden rake (or a potato hook) to produce a fine tilth after a light forking. This may be preferred for the small plot.

Where there is really hard ground, say around a newly-built house, there's a lot to be said for using a rotary cultivator to break up the surface to prepare it for seed sowing or planting. In some districts a machine may be hired. If the rototiller is small enough and narrow enough, not only can it prepare the ground for the vegetables, but in addition it can run down in between the rows of crops in order to control any weeds there may be later on. For this reason I always advise the spacing of the rows at either 18in or 3ft, for then a machine can travel down once between the 18in rows and twice between the 3ft rows, without doing any damage to the vegetables.

Mechanical cultivators come in several varieties with considerable differences in price. You must match the job to the cultivator and to your financial means. For a large plot you need more horsepower than for the smaller plot, and it seems that larger motors last longer than smaller ones so it can be worth the extra money to get the slightly larger model. You also have to decide between the rototillers which pull themselves along with their blades and those which run on power-driven wheels and drag their blades behind them. The latter are probably easier to manoeuvre but are more expensive. A point to remember is that after you get your garden well composted you will use your rototiller less and less, except in the vegetable plot.

LAWN MOWING

There is no doubt that the most effective way of mowing a town lawn and giving perfect grooming is to use a battery-electric reel-type lawn mower. This should have a dual drive so that it is fully self-propelled most of the time but can, by one simple movement, have the drive transferred to the cutting cylinder only. There should be a self-sharpening five-bladed steel cutting cylinder giving eighteen cuts per foot. No wrenches for adjusting the height of cut should be needed. There should also be a single 'on' and 'off' control lever on the handle. An unbreakable steel roller would allow you to cut the edges of borders and would give that immaculate striped effect which is so much liked. Of course weather in England promotes perfect grass which can take on that golf green look. In most of North America the problems that lawns present eventually force one to compromise. The most popular mower is the rotary type. These come with either motors, batteries or cords which plug directly into your electrical system. They can be hand-driven, self-propelled, or ridden. The ultimate machines are small tractors which have attachments which do most of your garden chores as well as mow your lawn. The equipment you decide upon will again depend on your needs and your finances. Whatever you choose, do not cut the grass shorter than $\frac{3}{4}$in from soil level.

Strong disease-resistant growth achieved by the use of compost (*Bernard Alfieri*)

A theory that has long been advanced by 'organic' gardeners is that grass cuttings can be utilised as a form of nutriment for the lawn from which they came. This is becoming more widely accepted. That grass cuttings make a valuable addition to the compost heap has long been known. But light and regular cutting of a lawn also enables the cuttings to be mulched and directly returned to the lawn as a form of nutriment. Another aspect to this is that so many gardeners prefer to save the time and effort spent on pushing cuttings to the compost pile by leaving them on the lawn. It has been estimated that up to one-third of the time spent in cutting a lawn is taken up by the emptying of the grassbox! At the same time, it must be accepted that if a lawn is left uncut too long, each mowing will leave a thick mat of cuttings over it and thus restrict growth or at least look unsightly. The riding or hover rotary mower has several advantages. It is easy to use and requires minimal exertion so the lawn gets cut more often. The rotor mulches the grass as it cuts and tends to spread the grass out when dry.

Whatever mower is used, a lawn should be raked and spiked several times a year for best results. One of the dangers of lawn cutting is to set the blades too low, 'scalping' the grass and thereby damaging the roots which should be promoting a rich, luxuriant growth. It also encourages the growth and spread of weeds, especially clover, crab grass and couch grass. A lawn can be likened in some ways to a man's beard. Every daily shaver knows that regular cutting stimulates the growth of his beard, but if he leaves off shaving for a few days the growth slows down and an unkempt appearance is the result. Light cutting of a lawn every three to five days is recommended for really luxuriant grass, not the once-a-fortnight onslaught which happens in many homes. By using modern techniques regular cutting of grass can be achieved with little effort. For cutting grass in odd inaccessible corners, incidentally, or close to walls and trees, there are small electric trimmers on handles which are light and easy to handle.

EDGES AND HEDGES

The other jobs for which mechanical aids are needed are cutting lawn edges and hedge trimming. There are machines which give a beautiful clean cut to lawn edges at any speed the gardener cares to walk. They have high-speed blades set at right angles to the lawn which chop the clippings so finely that they do not usually need to be picked up. The blade is generally exposed and therefore dangerous to the unwary. Take great care using any of these mechanical devices especially if you have pets or children who might wish to help.

Most hedges need cutting twice a year, in late spring and late summer or early autumn. As this can be a boring job, it is one of the reasons why I strongly recommend the use of a fence. Larch for instance is a long-lasting beautiful wood, and a larch-plank fence gives a great deal of pleasure, saves a lot of work and lasts a long time. Green hedges, however, are very attractive indeed, form an ideal background for flower borders, and can after all be cut mechanically with an electric machine. This will do the work four times as quickly as trying to cut by hand with a pair of shears.

WEEDING

The two types of weeds that the gardener has to cope with are perennials like thistles, nettles, dandelions and convolvulus, whose roots go deep into the ground and which come up year after year willy-nilly, and the annual weeds which arise from seeds sown this year or maybe from seeds sown fifty years back. These two types of weeds have to be treated in a totally different manner.

The *annual* weeds springing from seeds present in the soil are disturbed every time the gardener hoes to keep them down; thousands more start to grow in consequence! The more, therefore, you hoe to control the weeds, the more weed seeds are brought to the surface. With the compost-mulching system already described, no weed-seed disturbance occurs at all. The compost or peat humus sits on the surface of the ground and prevents the annuals from growing.

The *perennial* weeds which may infest gardens include dandelions, thistles, sweet clover, docks, couch grass, convolvulus (bindweed). They can all be controlled, but in some cases you need a good deal of patience and a fair amount of time.

A gardener who wishes to adopt the no-digging, no-forking, no-hoeing plus mulching methods must get rid of all perennial weeds first. It pays again and again to spend months completely eliminating the weeds before starting a new garden, or reclaiming an old one.

There are, of course, weed killers. These work in several ways. Some kill everything growing in the soil, while others are selective as to which family of plants they eliminate. It is somewhat out of the spirit of compost gardening to use poisons, but there are those who feel that weed killers are the only way to make their garden free from perennial weeds. If you must use one, choose from the selective poisons which work by direct application to the weed in question. For instance, there are weed killers which kill plants by attacking the chlorophyll (green colouring matter) in the leaves. In order to eliminate plants that are not needed or not wanted, the leaves have to be watered or sprayed with the poisons when in full growth. If the weeds are growing very strongly, and are firmly established, they sometimes need two or three waterings, at intervals of a month or so, to obtain the desired effect.

Part of the long herbaceous border at Arkley; the soil has never been dug, forked or hoed (*Pat Thomas*)

To eliminate perennial weeds without poisons takes time and understanding. Perennial plants grow each year from the same root system as well as from offshoots and seeds. The seeds are no problem once you have adopted the compost method, for the compost acts as a mulch preventing the seeds from germinating. It is the root system that remains and causes problems by poking up plants in spite of the mulch. The perennials which make up the herbaceous border do exactly the same thing as the perennial weeds but we want the perennial flowers and are pleased by their yearly appearance. To eliminate the weeds you must eliminate their root systems. Those which grow from a central bud or those which grow from a bulb are the easiest to root up for once the bulb or bud is gone the plant cannot reappear. It is the plants which grow from a fleshy tap root such as the dandelion or those which thrust out long underground roots called rhizomes from which new plants grow that cause the major problem.

In order to get rid of these weeds you must try to dig out all the roots but, better still, smother the plant with a impenetrable 6in deep mulch—if you can wait a full season before starting your garden. One approach is to start your preparation in the autumn by breaking up the surface soil to a depth of 2–3in with a mechanical cultivator. Mulch the area deeply with any organic material available (old hay, leaves, straw, newspaper, etc) and add some *organic* fertiliser at 4oz to the square yard. Thus composting is done on the site during the winter and early spring, leaving your plot with a layer of material which should discourage all annual weeds. The perennial weeds will, however, show themselves in the spring. Then you must attack the perennial weeds and eliminate them completely. Weeds such as dock or dandelion are treated with dry powdered sodium chlorate, which is carried down to the fleshy tap roots and kills the plants for good. If you try to dig or pull up these plants, you are bound to leave some root. You will find that the soil is much easier to work in for having had the 6in deep mulch cover during the winter. Weeds such as couch or quack grass grow nasty long runner roots which have nodes every few inches sending up new plants. These plants pull up quite easily but break at the node, leaving the node to send up its plant and send out more runners. Therefore it is best to kill them with a selective weed killer. Once you rid your garden of the grass you will find it trying to creep in from the sides. Some people have found that the grass will not cross a trench about 6in in depth, while others use plants such as marigolds or potatoes which seem to repel the grass together with other weeds of a similar growth pattern.

I must mention two annual weeds which might just invade your garden. In the United States common purslane (*Portulaca oleracea* L.) looks and acts like a low flat-growing succulent with a reddish stem, thickened rounded leaves and small yellow flowers. The plant reproduces by seed and by the rooting of bits of stem. If you find one of these plants in your garden be careful to remove it intact for any small bits accidentally dropped take root in the moist compost or peat humus covering your garden. In Britain, convolvulus is difficult because the stems twine around other plants, and so if you attempt to kill one you kill the other. It's best, therefore, to dip the tips of the plants, when they are 6in or so out of the soil, into weedkiller which can be held conveniently in a small tin or cup. This is the most tedious of all the operations, but is far better than attempting to dig the roots out of the soil, when you invariably leave tiny pieces in the ground to grow again.

USING 'LOVERS AND HATERS' TO HELP WITH THE WEEDS

Some recent investigations indicate that certain plants will deter the growth of other, unwanted plants. The Good Gardeners' Association, which carries out simple practical research, has tried out one of the tagetes, *Tagetes minuta*. This plant seems to have the power of driving away ground elder, couch grass and even convolvulus (bindweed). Unfortunately, this particular tagetes grows very tall, between 5 and 6ft in the Arkley Manor Gardens, though the plants did not need much staking, being firm 'on their feet'. The seeds can be sown where the plants are to grow, about the middle of April; or the sowing may be done in boxes filled with a seed-starting medium. The boxes are put into the greenhouse on the staging at a temperature of 55° F, and when the seedlings are an inch high they should be pricked out, preferably into 3in peat pots; these can go back on to the staging of the greenhouse to grow on, until in, say, three weeks' time they can go out into a frame for hardening off. When the weather is warmer, ie when all fear of frost is past, the plants may be put out where they are to grow, about 1ft or 18in apart.

Some readers may have trouble from neighbours who do no gardening at all. Thus all the pernicious perennial weeds creep through the bottom of the fencing or wire-netting from next door. The plan in this case has been to plant a whole row of *Tagetes minuta* right along the edge of the garden. This has generally been successful. It is claimed also that when tagetes is properly composted it can drive out the harmful eelworms in the soil. So far the research at Arkley Manor has shown that three perennial weeds—couch (or twitch or scutch), ground elder, and creeping buttercup—can be kept at bay with this plant. It is also excellent on the compost heap. Sow the seeds outdoors where you want the plants to grow, in mid-May, or—better still—raise the plants in the greenhouse or frame by sowing seeds there in mid-March. Plant out 8in apart in mid-May.

A Dutch horticulturist maintains that another type of 'African marigold', Colorado Sunshine (*Tagetes erecta*), completely killed the eelworm which ruined his daffodil bulbs, and the French marigold (*Tagetes patula*) can do the same.

Peas and beans, I find, seem to hate shallots, garlic or chives—so don't plant them near together. On the other hand, turnips and carrots love the three oniony crops—so grow them together. Some of my friends have had success in keeping away carrot-fly maggots by growing onions or leeks between the rows. Then, is it true that members of the pulse family—peas and beans—will not grow within 50ft of gladioli? I know it is true that moles will not come within 60yd of the caper spurge. Audrey Hatfield, in her book *How to Enjoy Your Weeds*, tells how she discovered that tomatoes will drive away couch or twitch grass. I discovered in the Wirral area of Cheshire that early potatoes when well fed with compost could and did drive away couch grass. The interesting thing is that the tomato and the potato are both members of the Solanaceae family.

It is usually said that roses should be planted on their own, but I have known them flourish extraordinarily well with parsley planted as an under crop. It is reported however, that roses prefer onions above all. These can be given as an 'onion-waste' mulch with success it seems, so use the outside skins of your onions on top of the bed; it is undoubtedly the volatile sulphur given off by the onion which prevents the black-spot disease.

For years I have been studying plant partnerships, and again a few definite findings emerge. The mycorrhiza on the roots of heathers benefit the mycorrhiza on the roots of conifers; French or snap beans and cucumbers are 'friends'—they both crop better when grown next to one another; lettuces are first-class friendly intercrops for carrots or parsnips; and runner or pole beans and brussels sprouts are a good pair together.

It has been said that climbing types of nasturtium grown around the base of apple trees will prevent their being attacked by woolly aphides; some people have had good results by adopting this method—others have failed. And turning to animal pests, we have found that an effective way of deterring moles from tunnelling under lawns and crops is to plant caper spurge: this is discussed more fully in the section on pests and diseases, p 108.

WATERING

Because the compost gardener covers his soil with a mulch of compost the moisture in the soil is largely conserved and is not 'drawn out' by the sun and whisked away by the wind. However, in very dry summers watering may be necessary in the case of lawns and vegetable gardens. Trees and shrubs may suffer too, because of excessive transpiration by the leaves. (Transpiration is a loss of moisture through the pores, like sweating in human beings.) Though the sun cannot dry out the soil of a compost garden, the roots of plants can take up literally gallons of water in order to keep the leaves turgid (ie firm) and cool. So when the leaves of shrubs and trees start to droop, water must be given. This rule also applies to a herbaceous border or a cut-flower garden, an iris garden, a red-hot poker bed, or what have you.

Never attempt, however, to give water by means of a watering can. The compost gardener must use an overhead sprinkler on the end of a hose, and this artificial rain-giver must remain in one position for at least three-quarters of an hour so that sufficient water will be applied to soak the ground properly—as a good rainfall would naturally. Another important advantage in using what is sometimes called a 'rainer' is that the little drops of water are thrown up into the air and so get slightly aerated. It is this aeration which takes place when rail falls that ensures that no scorching takes place on the leaves of the plants. So always use a rainer that throws the water up as high as possible so that it falls on the plants and the soil like natural rain. In this way the best results are achieved.

In the vegetable garden it is a good thing to apply the artificial rain (by the way, this is the only artificial thing the compost gardener uses) once a week on sandy soils, or once a fortnight on clays, in a dry summer. If there is a substantial shower during any seven-day period the overhead irrigation will be unnecessary. In the case of vegetables, and particularly with salads which consist of 90 per cent water, artificial rain should be given for an hour in one spot—so

Well-cropped organic vegetable garden (*Harry Smith*)

that the equivalent of, say, half-an-inch of rain is applied. In desert areas ditch irrigation may be necessary. To learn this technique consult local gardeners.

TOPPING UP THE COMPOST

You have spread the brown powdery compost or its equivalent peat humus 1in deep all over the levelled land in the flower and shrub garden etc, and it is left there as a top dressing or mulch.

As the worms work away, producing the necessary humus, they may pull in about a ¼in layer of compost. When this happens the gardener adds another layer all over the ground concerned. It is a simple matter to disturb the mulch layer to see how deep it is. There is no need to do so until about six months after the original application. Six months later a second application may be made. Usually after two years and certainly after three or four the worms will have pulled in all the organic matter they need in bulk, and thus the 1in layer of compost on the ground will not be disturbed. At the Arkley Manor Gardens, Herts, I have rose beds which have not been hoed for eight years, and no compost has had to be added during that period. So it can be said that one has to top up for a year or two, depending on the humus content of the soil when one starts on the no-digging, no-forking method.

If a gardener is able to choose the time of the very first application of compost or peat humus, it should be mid-April or early May, ie just as the soil is warming up again. Level the soil in the bed first; if this is not done, then the 1in mulch cannot, of course, be put on level, and the upper part of the uneven soil may eventually be exposed, allowing the weed seeds in that area to germinate and grow.

ORGANIC FEEDING

Generally speaking one can say that when compost is made properly, from differing types of organic matter such as one can collect from any garden and home, it contains all the necessary foods needed by the plants; it will include not only the macro-nutrients (the major plant foods) but the micro-nutrients as well. Thus there are many good gardeners who grow vegetables, fruit and flowers with their own good brown powdery compost alone. However, as mentioned in Chapter 2 there is nothing wrong in giving the soil an organically based fertiliser like meat and bone meal, hoof and horn meal, fish manure, or seaweed manure. The adding of such natural fertilisers to the soil can be looked on as giving the plants a tonic. For instance, after a very cold winter, roses and other plants can be encouraged by applying dried blood at, say, 1oz to the square yard or a fish manure at 2oz to the square yard. This extra feed will help the millions of bacteria to do the work that they are intended to do.

4

TAKING OVER A DERELICT OR A BRAND-NEW GARDEN

TO get an old or a new garden going properly is a less alarming prospect for the compost gardener than for the bastard-trenching and double-digging addict. Virtually the first job will have to be the construction of the compost bins, as described in Chapter 2, as all the overgrown vegetation that has to be cleared should go to make the compost such gardens urgently need. Until you have some good compost, you will in any case be spending money on peat humus or a substitute.

THE DERELICT GARDEN

It is difficult, of course, to envisage every type of derelict garden that may be found all round the world, but from my long experience as a horticultural adviser, I can imagine the worst.

The hedges are invariably overgrown, and a priority job is to cut them back hard on one side, the side facing inwards, to help increase the garden's light and air and to make more room. It is always better to cut one side hard back one year, and the other the next year. If the hedge has grown too tall, then the top must be cut to leave it, say, 6ft high—which is normally good enough to prevent the prying eyes of neighbours seeing in, if you like your privacy. The hedge prunings, being woody, will be burnt, and the ashes then put on the compost heap a little at a time, increasing the heap's potash content.

The base of the hedge may be full of rubbish and so is a breeding ground for pests. All the debris should therefore be raked or hoed away; as this—as a rule—is organic, it can go on the compost heap to be treated with an activator such as fish manure, seaweed manure or poultry manure. Now apply one of these organic fertilisers along the bottom of the hedge at 4oz to the yard run: it is 100 to 1 that the hedge has not been fed for many years and will benefit greatly from this.

Fruit

Having tackled the hedges, go for the soft fruit bushes and canes. If the black currants are covered with 'big buds' swollen buds four or five times the size of the ordinary buds, some of which you are sure to see on the young wood, then they are not worth keeping and can be grubbed up for burning. The red currants you can tell from the black currants by the absence of the curranty smell if you rub your hand along a branch: try it on a black currant branch first and you will see what I mean. All that needs to be done with healthy currants is to prune them, and this is done by cutting out the centre of the bush to leave it goblet shaped and then

Compost bins at Arkley Manor, showing one bin being filled and a second ready for use. (*Author*)

Compost in use at Arkley Manor on the annual cut flower border.
(*Author*)

Strawberry – Talisman. (*Harry Smith*)

cutting back all the one-year-old side-growths to within half an inch of the base. The end one-year-old growths on each branch will be cut back by half to just above an outward-growing bud. The wood you cut off will be burnt, and the ashes brought back afterwards and sprinkled among the currant bushes because they will appreciate extra potash.

If there are gooseberries or blueberries, these will need thinning out to remove the crossing wood, the rubbing wood and all branches that are drooping on the ground. When you have finished cutting out all the old and new wood that is crowding up the centre, it should be possible to get your hand anywhere among the branches without getting scratched.

Raspberries are often a problem, because if they have been neglected it is certain the ripe berries will have dropped to the ground, that the seeds in them will have germinated in the soil and that young seedling canes will have grown up. These are invariably *useless*: they are strong and appear healthy, but they produce appalling one-sided berries as a rule. My advice there is to dig up all the raspberry canes and burn them. Once again the ash can come back on to the soil if it is your idea to plant new canes in that same position.

Any strawberries will almost certainly have to come out. It is never worthwhile trying to keep an old overgrown strawberry bed. The plants will be full of virus, so before planting new healthy stocks of strawberries be sure to get up the old beds and compost all the plants and runners therein. By treating them with an activator, the viruses will be killed and a beautiful powdery compost result.

Fruit trees can be a problem. They are usually of three kinds: (a) very tall, very difficult to get at, standard; (b) overgrown thickets of dwarf trees; or (c) ruined espaliers or fan-trained wall or fence trees.

The value of any standard will have to be weighed up carefully. If there is a specimen tree that might be used as a feature in the garden, perhaps with a semi-circular seat around it, then keep it—not so much for its fruit as for its beauty of outline. The branches could probably be thinned out a little here and there so as to let in the light and air. If the trees are old and diseased then they may be sawn down to soil level and the stumps treated to rot them away. Big trees to be cut down, by the way, are best pollarded first and then the tops can be sawn off, leaving a straight trunk before the sawing at soil level is done. This saves doing any damage to a green-house or the rest of the garden.

Dwarf trees are often worth keeping, unless they are in the wrong position. Get rid of them, for instance, if they are in the part of the garden you plan to use for vegetables—because the two do not go well together.

The bushes you wish to keep will be thinned out here and there, so as to let in the light and air and remove the crossing or rubbing branches and the diseased wood. The espalier trees will have to be pruned so as to reduce the length of the spurs, as they are called, and readers who have to tackle such trees will do well to consult books covering the subject in detail, including my own—*The A.B.C. of Fruit Growing* and *The A.B.C. of Pruning.*

Weeds

Weed control has been described in Chapter 3. The perennial weeds, the docks, dandelions, thistles, ground elder and the like, should be tackled firmly as discussed there, but the annual weeds, such as crab grass, pigweed, or chickweed, can be hoed off and put on the compost heap —they make marvellous compost.

Planning the garden

Once some order has been created, the rubbish has been cleared, the hedges cut and the weeds eliminated, then the gardener must settle down to planning a minimum-work compost garden. Take the trouble to draw it out on a sheet of squared paper. *Do not* try to make the whole garden as you want it in one year—get your priorities right and then work to, say, a three-year plan.

It may be possible to follow the lines of the original garden, but if it is many years old, it will probably be far too fussy. For instance, there may be flower beds, round, crescent-shaped, and square, cut out of the lawn: get rid of them by grassing them over. Have the fruit plot on its own so that you can spray the trees without injuring other plants; and bear in mind that it is nice to see the beauty of the garden from the house windows, so don't plant trees and bushes too close to them—leave yourself a lovely view. Once you have decided what you want to grow, and whether, for instance, you can retain the old herbaceous border, just digging it over, splitting the plants and replanting the best parts, you can cover your cultivated areas with their layer of compost. The lawn can then be raked, spiked, treated with hormones to get rid of the weeds and of course also fed with compost.

The heather garden at Arkley (*author*)

THE BRAND-NEW GARDEN

The house has probably been built on an old pasture. The builders will have made quite a mess of the area near the house, but something like the remaining three-quarters of it is likely to be rough grass. Once the builders' brickbats and rubbish have been removed, what is the compost gardener going to do? Well, one thing he isn't going to do is to dig the land over and bury the turf trench by trench, as most uninformed people do.

Most of the area will not be disturbed at all, except for any necessary levelling. With a new garden you can really let yourself go over the planning, and do what you like. Decide what you want to grow and aim to satisfy your own wishes. The overall effect to aim at is one of spaciousness with some sort of vista—a looking beyond. So keep any herbaceous and shrub borders to the sides of the garden, perhaps having a lovely long lawn down the centre. The borders down each side may curve round to help produce the vista effect, and also to help to hide the utilitarian part of the garden that can be set beyond, as well as providing a focal point. The simple plan (p 43) shows what I mean. This can be varied to suit your needs, but it does emphasise the general principles to be borne in mind.

If you like heathers, and in non-alkaline soils these are easy to cultivate, have a heather garden. If flowering shrubs are your ideal, aim for a beautiful shrub border—which, if mulched with compost, will take the absolute minimum of looking after. If vegetables are to be grown, choose a spot away from trees, as sunny as possible, and see to it that the compost heaps are nearby so that there will not be too much carting about from one area to the other. I don't mind seeing the vegetables myself, but if you think them ugly and utilitarian, they may be hidden by a pretty hedge, such as a row of the prunus 'Blaze', or even a rose hedge of strong floribundas.

The area to be devoted to vegetables will be forked over lightly in order to incorporate the grass turf into the top 2 or 3in of soil. Those who have or can hire a rototiller should use this. After the shallow cultivation the powdery compost is spread on top. It is necessay to be generous and use the powdery compost, either home-made or natural (ie peat humus), at the rate of two good wheelbarrow loads to 10 square yards.

It is in this prepared soil that the seeds are sown or the plants put in. A feed of fish manure or meat and bone meal, or even hoof and horn meal, at 3oz to the square yard, can be applied when the land is being raked level. If the ground is known to be acid, carbonate of lime can be added as a *top dressing* at, say, 6–7oz to the square yard, especially on the parts to be used for the peas and beans and brassicas. Don't use lime on the part used for potatoes and root crops.

Part of your rough area will be turned into a lawn just by the method of regular spiking, rolling and cutting the grass weekly and, of course, eliminating the weeds with a hormone liquid. The lawn as it is being cut will be fed with compost or a sewage sludge fertiliser to improve the turf. Thus the lawn will be produced with the minimum of effort.

If you want herbaceous borders, prepare the land concerned as for the vegetable plot and insert the plants in accordance with the scheme you have drawn up. In the land round the house that has been disturbed by the builders, fork and rake level, even though some subsoil has been brought to the top. Once the soil is reasonably level spread compost all over it to encourage the worms to start working, so that they do the digging for you and start to prepare a humus-filled surface soil. Such plants as dwarf dahlias, geraniums, salvias and violas can be planted in summer followed, by wallflowers, forget-me-nots and bulbs for the winter and spring.

If part of the garden is to be used for apples, pears and plums, these will be planted in the turf with say, a 10 or 12ft square for each tree. Holes will be made in the grass about 2ft across and 6in deep—just sufficient to take the roots of the trees which must be well spread out. The grass sods are then put back in the hole upside down exactly as they came out. Thus all that has to be done in the future is to keep the grass cut with a rotary mower and allow the grass to lie where it falls, so that the worms can pull it in.

The soft fruits too can be planted in the grass. Make the rows 6ft apart and plant the bushes

5ft apart in the rows and the canes 2ft apart. The only ground that must be prepared is a narrow strip 18in wide, lightly forked over so that the bushes or canes can be planted. The grass in between the rows is cut with a rotary mower and the grass mowings can be raked in the rows so as to smother the grass growing there. Thus the soft fruits will be grown in a lawn.

Part of the pasture in this new garden can be used to form what I call a 'Henry VIIIth garden'. All that has to be done in this case is to plant flowering shrubs—preferably the genuinely old-fashioned ones—in the grass rather in the same way as the fruit trees except that they are *not* planted in straight lines. The idea is to cut a grass path with an ordinary mower, wandering in and out of the shrubs, and in at least two places have a nice elm seat made without nails—ie with wedges—for sitting in the sun or the shade. The grass under the shrubs can be cut with a rotary mower and left 2in or more long, while the path is cut shorter, down to 1in.

So, with the new area used intelligently and carefully, you can in a year or two create a beautiful and healthy garden, to give pleasure and little work year by year.

5

THE TOWN GARDEN

IT is seldom that one sees an adequate front garden in the middle of a town or city; they are the exception rather than the rule. Many town and city gardens on the other hand have a good back garden or back yard, even if the owners do call it the 'cat run' or the 'rat run'. Sometimes the area seems only just a yard wide since it is long and narrow with high walls on either side, occasionally there are huge trees, either in the garden itself or growing next door, which provide so much shade and so severely rob the soil that the growing of plants is made difficult indeed.

THE SOIL

It is necessary to approach a town garden with several thoughts in mind. The first is that the soil will undoubtedly be very poor—or as one gardener put it to me, 'as poor as Lazarus'. It has been a garden perhaps for generations, nobody has attempted to feed the soil, and so the earth is completely eroded and the poor householder is having to deal with something resembling a black desert sand. Alternatively, and this is particularly true of some riverside cities, the soil may be composed almost entirely of a horrible buttery, bluey or yellowy clay. This has never been given a chance of improving itself and sometimes the soil drainage is so bad that the earth remains permanently sodden.

As the roots of the plants have to dwell in the soil, and as 75 per cent of most plants is below ground and only 25 per cent above ground, the prospective town or city gardener must be prepared to be liberal with the addition of organic matter and organic plant foods. Both the powdery soil and the sticky soil need humus. Humus will darken soil; it will open up heavy clays, it will bind together sands, it will provide the soil bacteria with what they need. As already said, it cannot be applied to the ground, the organic matter from which it is made, compost or peat humus, being what is needed. Use two or three bucketsful to the square yard. The addition of a fish fertiliser will supply all the plant foods necessary, including the three main ones, nitrogen, phosphates and potash, and in addition all kinds of minor plant-food elements which may be lacking in town soil. Use the fish manure at 2 to 4oz per square yard.

There is also the chance in a town garden that the soil is very acid and has not been limed for years. The garden owner, therefore, is well advised to make a simple test in order to determine roughly how much lime is needed. Lime not only corrects acidity but adds calcium, an important plant food. Lime very quickly washes through soil and should, therefore, always be applied on the surface of the ground and not dug in. Those who are adopting the peat humus mulching method will give a heavy dressing of lime to the surface of the soil after the first lot of compost or peat humus has been worked in.

Foliage and flowering plants in a small town garden (*Harry Smith*)

Lime should never be mixed with the fish fertiliser and must be applied alone. In the ordinary way I use it at about 8oz to the square yard, in town gardens found to be acid, and for the purpose either hydrated lime or carbonate of lime will do the job. Most garden centres have acidity-testing paper strips on sale, the paper giving an easily recognisable colour for each important lime level. You turn over the top 2in of soil with a trowel, and mix a level teaspoonful of this moist soil with one teaspoonful of tap water in a saucer. After half-an-hour place the strip so that half of it lies on top of the wet soil and the other half against the saucer. After five minutes, compare the colour of the portion of paper lying against the saucer with the colour panels on the chart provided with the test papers. Thus you know the correct amount of lime to apply.

THE TREES

Sunlight is the most basic requirement of all for plant growth. Leaves, the great manufacturing centres of the plants, produce starches and sugars from the light received, passing them down in the sap to make new roots and passing them to the seeds or fruits to make them larger and perhaps more succulent. It is therefore important for garden plants to receive as much sunlight as possible, and in a town garden the amount can easily be inadequate. Trees planted years ago may have become too large for their position and overhang too far—and incidentally their roots, in trying to grow, compete with those of other plants, the latter invariably suffering in the competition. Often, too, there are tall buildings nearby. Many city gardens have high brick walls around them, which though excellent at giving privacy do bar the sunlight.

Trees in a small back garden should be used with care. Some people get over the difficulty by planting a tree in a large tub or barrel so that firstly its roots are restricted, and secondly it can easily be removed after, say, ten years or so, when it has grown unwieldy and sheds too much shade. Others minimise the problem by planting fastigiate trees, those that grow like a church spire and never spread out. *Cupressus fastigiata* is typical, or the Japanese cherry Amanogawa, which has fragrant semi-double soft pink flowers. There are also, of course, many dainty trees with less damaging roots and less dense foliage. The Japanese maples, for instance, are noted for the rich autumn colours of their leaves, the most brilliant probably being *Acer palmatum* osakazuki.

When there are trees already in the garden, one or two could be cut down to soil level, the stumps then being treated to rot them quickly in situ. If a tree is left, it may be possible to put a circular seat round it, with some circular paving, and make it a focal point. If necessary, some of the lower branches can be sawn back to reduce the amount of shade; if this is done the saw cuts should be made as close to the main stem as possible, and the surfaces of the cuts should be smoothed up afterwards with the sharper blade of a knife and painted with a lead paint, preferably grey or brown. Only a good lead paint will keep out the spores of diseases.

Sometimes it is the next-door neighbour who has all the trees, and he may not be keen on pruning them intelligently because of the time and labour required; but you can saw off carefully all the branches that are overhanging your garden. The legal aspect of this is clear: you should firstly write to the garden owner and ask him to cut back the branches that stray on to your side of the boundary. If he refuses to do so, you write to him again politely, and say that you will be cutting them off at a joint just above your hedge, fence or wall, and that having given him due warning, there is nothing he can do about it; if there is any fruit on the branches at the time of the sawing, you should give your neighbour the opportunity of picking it up, as this is not specifically yours. Laws concerning the air space above your land are fairly universal, but I strongly recommend that you consult your local authorities or your lawyer before trimming your neighbour's tree.

If the tree or trees are yours, you may of course with long ladders and saws do the necessary pruning work yourself; but if you are frightened of doing this because of the height, or because you are not sure of the method, it is possible to employ special tree surgeons who will do the work expeditiously and, if desired, take the log wood away. If preferred, they will log up the branches and leave them for you to burn.

REFLECTED LIGHT

Having made certain that there is the minimum of shade and drip from trees, it is now necessary to do everything possible to provide reflected light. It is surprising how tremendously valuable reflected light can be; a room, for instance, may have a dark red or dark green wallpaper and look sombre and dull; paint its walls with a white, light blue, pale pink or light yellow paint and it will brighten in an extraordinary manner. Greenhouse owners who know what they are doing always cover the woodwork, staging, purlins and even water pipes with a glossy white paint in order to ensure the maximum reflected light. The same kind of thing holds good in the garden. Some people are horrified when told that the inside walls or fences should be whitewashed or painted white for the sake of the plants. For some, the shock isn't so severe when it is added that a light yellow distemper, or even what is called a sunlight colour will do. The wooden edgings to paths can be of similar light colour and so can the stakes used for trees, chrysanthemums or dahlias. If there is a frame in the garden, this should have glistening white sides both inside and out; that seat round a tree should also be white. Light tone paving brick or grey-white concrete slabs for the paths give far more reflected light than can paths made with red bricks, asphalt or a bituminous substance. These facts are emphasised for the really dark garden—the garden with tall walls round it, in a congested area with houses and factories on every side.

CATS

Cats are a notorious problem in town gardens. My own cat is well behaved, doesn't scratch up seedlings, and finds no need to ruin the trunks of trees with his claw-sharpening; preserve me, however, from the neighbours' cats that trouble some of my friends. They can ruin the bases of trees, they may sunbathe in the seedling beds, they can scratch up soil galore in order 'to do their business'. They may chase one another and knock down plants; they also, of course, kill birds, some of which are already none too plentiful in towns. Be prepared to try and keep cats from ruining trees by surrounding the trunks with $\frac{1}{4}$in wire-netting, sufficiently loose to allow the trunk to grow—if the tree is a young one. You will find, too, that if you have a well-trained dog the cats won't visit your garden so much. A dog can always be trained to stick to the paths and the lawn—but please not a bitch, because she will ruin a small lawn very quickly indeed, by using it as and when nature calls.

THE SECLUDED GARDEN

A front garden is 'the unselfish garden', shared by all. It can be made beautiful and is enjoyed by the householder, but it gives equal pleasure to the passer-by. The garden at the back of the house is quite different. It is here that the owner can sit in privacy and really enjoy the fruits of his own labours. The children can play, the old folk can sit and get the benefit of the sunshine, and if it is argued that a man's house is his castle then surely it can be said that a man's back garden or yard is his demesne.

It has been my privilege to help in the designing of numbers of gardens, and the plan has always been to try to break away from the old-fashioned idea that you must have a lawn in the centre with two borders of equal size on either side, and then perhaps an odd bit of vegetable garden at the bottom.

Garden No 1

A slight breakaway, just sufficient to make all the difference and yet not upset those of us who like what is familiar, will be found in the plan (p 43).

The idea is to have a small lawn for the children to play on, with a herbaceous border on the left-hand side—note its wavy edge—and a narrow border for annuals or even bedding plants on the right-hand side. Nobody wants to have unnecessary work, and as the perennial border will need little looking after it should be given the primary place with the greatest amount of room; the annual border will be much narrower. It is always possible in such a border to adopt a simple bedding-out scheme, say wallflowers and tulips in the spring, or forget-me-nots and daffodils. These could be followed by displays of dwarf dahlias in the summer or salvias, zinnias, geraniums or any of the bedding-out plants that make a brilliant show during the hotter months. One has to face the fact that twice a year such a border needs forking over for replanting, and that unless the garden owner has a greenhouse in which plants can be raised it will be quite expensive to get all that are needed. That is why most people prefer annuals which can be grown in place, the seed being comparatively cheap to buy. There is only the sowing in the spring followed by the thinning out and hoeing, and there should be a wonderful show throughout the season.

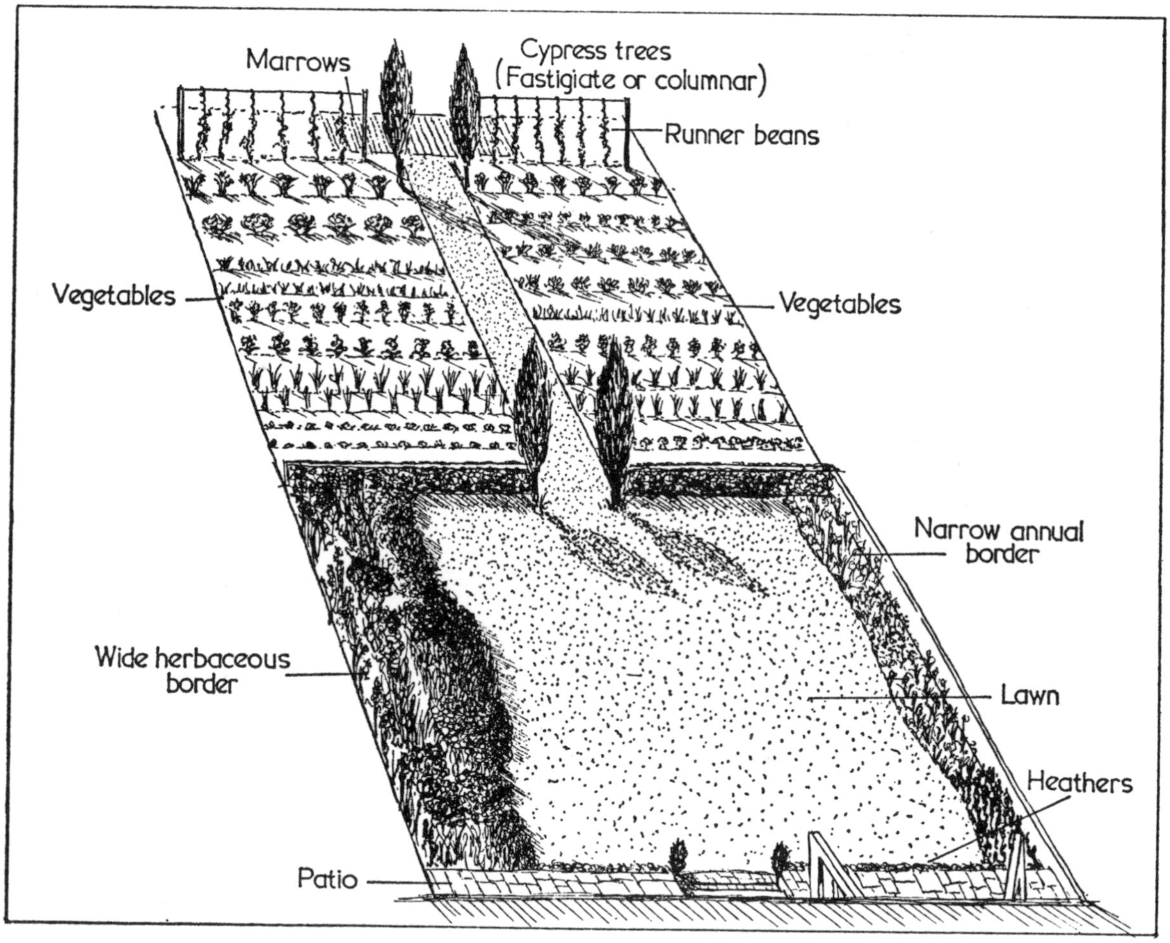

Compost-system garden design, 1

At the base of this part of the garden a lonicera or escallonia hedge is planted to divide the flowers and the lawn from the vegetable garden below. The main path has been kept opposite the french windows at the back of the house so that when sitting in the living-room, or standing on the steps, there is that long vista-like effect, which in these small gardens is so important to give the effect of distance. Right at the bottom of the path the seed bed could be conveniently situated.

It will help enhance this vista idea if two fastigiate cypress (cupressus) trees are planted as sentinels on either side of the path near the hedge and two more at the base of the path, that is to say on either side of the seed bed. The alternative is to have a row of cordon trees trained at an angle of 45° on either side of the path. Another idea is to have two conical-shaped box bushes growing in tubs at the base of the steps. Of course, in the vegetable garden—and this is important where there are children—the crops will be grown in standard rows. Plenty of compost will be applied as a top dressing (see p 37). Most families will concentrate on peas and beans, lettuce and tomatoes, plus greens for the winter as well as the spring. There may not be room in such a garden for potatoes or even for celery. Naturally, it depends on the length of the garden and on the size of the family, but in most cases these suggestions will hold good.

At the bottom of the garden it is possible to train runner or pole beans up the fence on one side and cucumbers, marrows or squashes on the other side. Few people realise that they can be grown in this way, but they much prefer being tied up the wires provided for the purpose than scrambling along the soil.

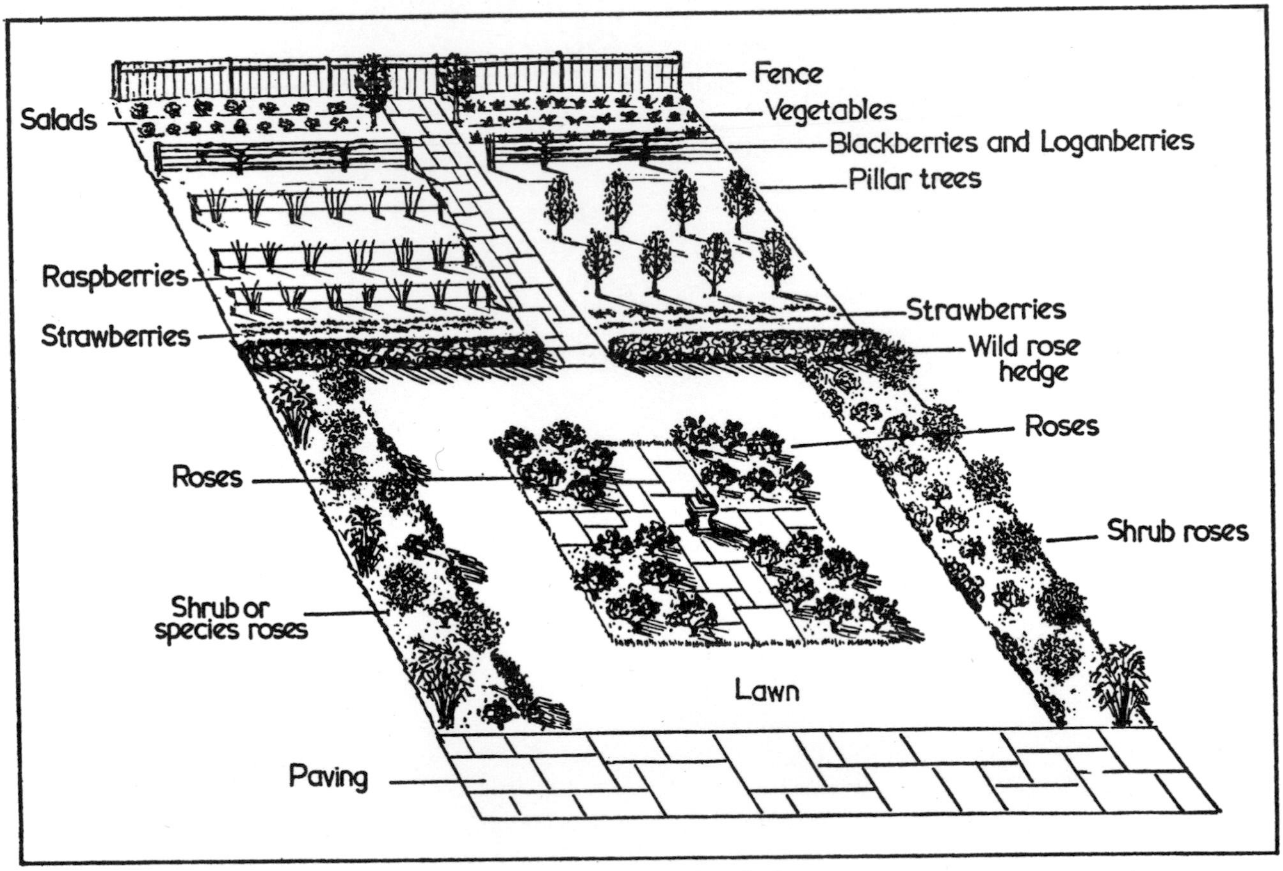

Compost-system garden design, 2

Garden No 2

I planned Garden No 2 (above) especially for a family that hated cutting grass. Paving blocks are used to form not only the terrace but the main path as well; these blocks fitting in splendidly with any type of house that is built. The four centre beds were devoted to roses, and because of the block surrounds we purposely stuck to the varieties with golden-yellow, white, orange and pink flowers like Anne Letts, Beauté, Barbara Richards, Betty Uprichard, Camellia Rose, Caroline Testout, Grandma Jenny, Guinevere, Ideal Home, Kings Ransom, Lady Seton, Monique, Rex Anderson, Innocence, White Swan, Silver Lining, Sterling Silver, Summer Sunshine and The Doctor.

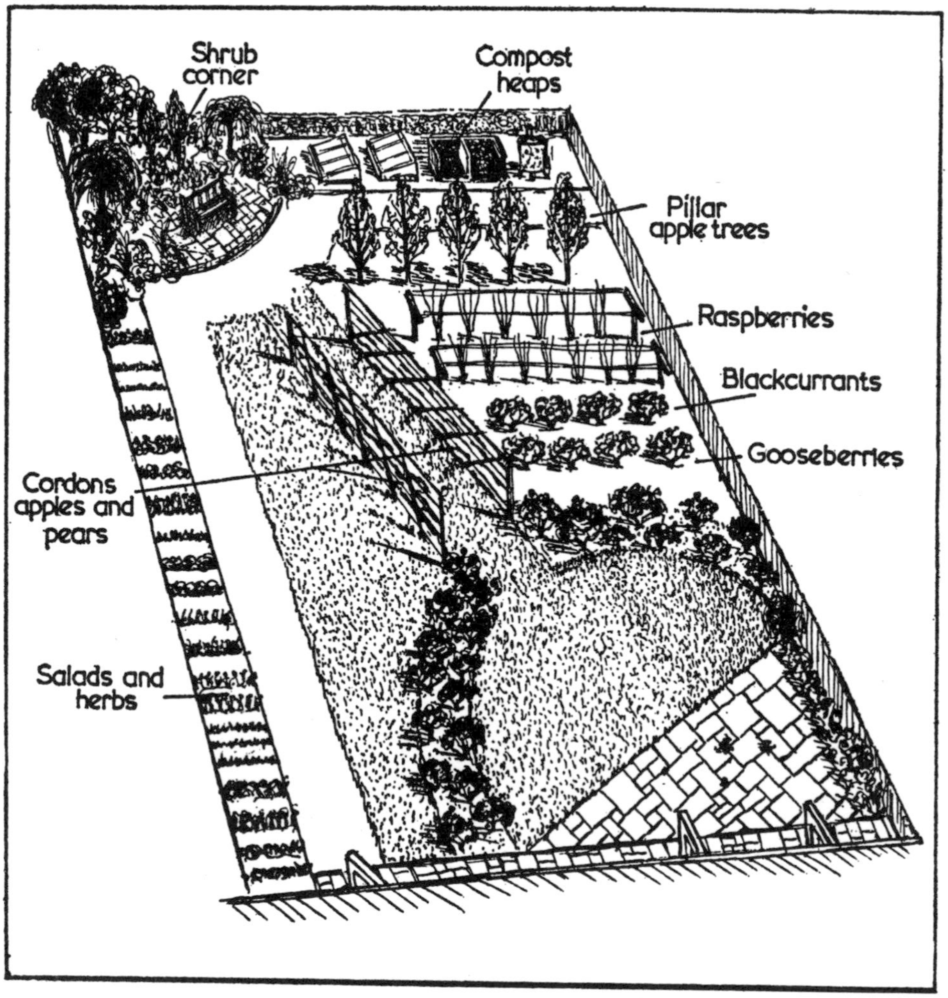

Another small garden design

On either side of these four beds the narrow borders were used for various shrub roses such as Crimson Damask, which is crimson and sweetly scented, Fruhlingsgold, cream with a golden centre, Hugonis with brilliant yellow single flowers, and Maiden's Blush with flesh-pink flowers with a darker centre, and very fragrant. They are very effective and take little looking after. The hedge used for dividing this formal garden from the vegetable and fruit garden below is sweet briar, which gives a very pleasant scent, especially in the evening hours and after rain.

If any owner is keen on fruit growing, then the planting of apple and pear trees on the pillar system is advisable. The trees in this garden were specially bought grafted on the Type

VII or MM 106 stock, with the result that they came into cropping very early and they never grew too large. They are specially planted on the right-hand side so as to make it easier for spraying.

The two small lower plots behind the trained cane fruits can be used almost entirely for salads that could be eaten raw—lettuce, ridge cucumbers, tomatoes, endive, spring onions, parsley, thyme and mint, stringless French or green beans, Mangetout or snow peas, and a row or two of cabbage, grown expressly for their white hearts. The division between the fruit and the salad quarters may consist of posts and wires, up which blackberries can be trained on one side and a loganberry on the other.

The lawn around the roses could be chamomile, the special plants needed for the purpose being the Treneage Strain. These are planted 6in apart and soon grow together to form a carpet which needs less mowing, which never goes to seed and which remains green all the year round. Those who don't care for chamomile (which is so successful in the Buckingham Palace gardens), can of course have an ordinary grass lawn.

6

THE FLOWER GARDEN

IN Victorian days there was a tremendous amount of what was called 'bedding-out'. This was the planting out of all kinds of hardy and half-hardy plants which would flower in the summer and early autumn. Then when these 'bedders' had finished their beautifying work the gardeners set about taking them up and putting in, instead, plants which would live through the winter and flower in the spring. Thus there was constant planting and replanting, and further, greenhouses had to be set aside for the raising of the plants thus needed; all work, and more work. However, the wealthier folk of those days had gardeners and didn't need to care; and in fact they loved the complicated geometrical designs produced by using plants with different-coloured leaves and flowers.

Today, when everyone anxious to have a beautiful garden with the minimum amount of work, bedding out is less and less popular, and so are the purely annual flower borders. People concentrate on flowering-shrub borders which are permanent; herbaceous borders which are semi-permanent; and roses which will go on flowering for years if they are looked after.

In this chapter, therefore, I have concentrated on these three main types of flower borders. All of them are perhaps more expensive to establish in the first place than bedding plants, but all work out far cheaper when their length of life is considered. Spend a sizeable sum on a shrub border and you have beauty for twenty years and more—so it costs you a mere fraction of that a year! Permanent and semi-permanent flower growing is in fact very rewarding indeed. It is no wonder that discerning amateur gardeners are finding these three methods of beautifying the land they own extremely satisfying in every way.

THE HERBACEOUS BORDER

The great advantage of the perennial is that it comes up year after year. It is expensive to buy, it is true, compared with the annual; but once you have it, it is there for good. Furthermore, the perennial as a rule increases in size, and the clump can be split up at the end of two or three years, thus making two or three plants; indeed, after a time this increase can prove almost an embarrassment.

There are perennial flowering plants of all kinds; tall ones, dwarf ones, climbers, scented kinds, solid kinds and dainty kinds; the herbaceous border, a border planted up with perennials of various kinds, can be one of the most pleasing features of any garden.

A perennial border should ideally be as wide as possible to get the best effect. In very large gardens these borders are often 12ft wide, but a 6ft or 9ft border in the normal garden is very effective, and I have borders in my own garden that are between 3 and 4ft wide and they look very well, too. Don't be put off from having a herbaceous border because you can't give it tremendous width. If you prefer your border can be curved instead of straight—so it can be somewhat wider in some parts than others. Remember, however, that the border is going to be down a number of years, so take great care in feeding the soil well.

Preparing and planting

Get rid of all the perennial weeds (if any) as advised in Chapters 1 and 4. The border must be free from such weeds before planting. Add powdery composted plant refuse or peat humus at

Delphinium (*Harry Smith*)

the rate of two good bucketsful to the square yard and see that it is incorporated in the top 2–3in. Leave the ground to settle and then, if the weather is dry, tread it well and get it firm. Before the plants go in apply a standard fish manure at 3–4oz per square yard, and fine wood ashes at the same rate. Rake these in lightly. Meat and bone meal can be used instead at 3–4oz to the square yard and has the advantage of feeding the roots as well as being slow-acting.

Finally, if the soil is known to be acid (see p 39), dress the surface of the ground with hydrated lime at about 5oz to the square yard.

Don't dig the border over first—plant in the undug soil. More plants are lost each year from being loosely planted than from any other reason. If you don't see that the roots are set firmly, then they may be in dry air-pockets and so will suffer. Remember that the roots have to take their food in solution, and they can only do this if the soil is properly tightened around them. Remember too that plants that are not firm may rock about in the soil and thus will not be able to throw out more roots to ensure good anchorage. Never double up the roots underneath the plants: make the hole large and deep enough for the roots to be spread out to their fullest extent. Once they are spread, put a little loose soil over the top and tread down, continuing to tread as the soil is filled in.

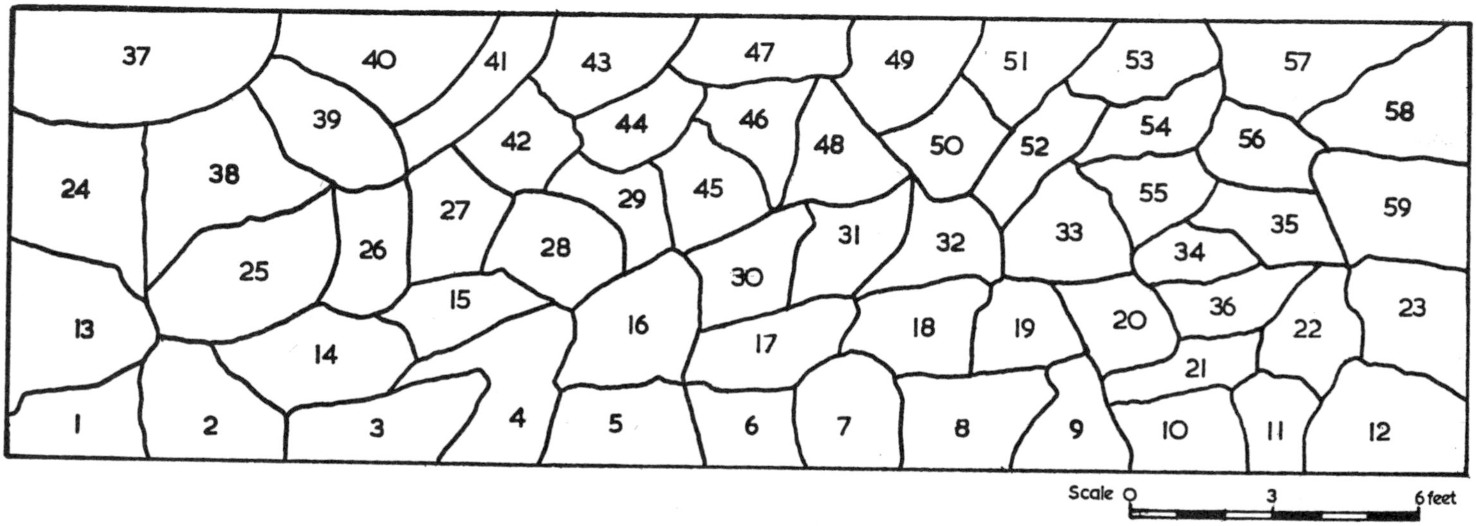

Herbaceous border chart

(1) Aster Nancy 9in
(2) Santolina incana 18in
(3) Tradescantia subaspera montana 2½ft
(4) Geranium pratense roseum 18in
(5) Veronica spicata barcarothe 2ft
(6) Tradescantia virginica Isis 18in
(7) Verbena corymbosa 18in
(8) Geum Lady Stratheden 18in
(9) Saponaria officinalis plena 2½ft
(10) Salvia hispanica 2ft
(11) Solididago Golden Thumb 12in
(12) Bergenia cordifolia 12in
(13) Sidalcea Puck 2ft
(14) Salvia ambigens 3ft
(15) Pyrethrum May Queen 2ft
(16) Ranunculus acris plenus 2ft
(17) Trollius baudirektor linne 2ft
(18) Pyrethrum Venus 2ft
(19) Ruta Jackman's blue 3ft
(20) Gaillardia aristata grandiflora 2ft
(21) Solidago Golden Falls 2ft
(22) Kniphofia Mount Etna 5ft
(23) Thalictrum dipterocarpum 4ft
(24) Papaver orientale Mrs Perry
(25) Solidago Golden Gates 3ft
(26) Scabiosa caucasica Clive Greaves 2ft
(27) Sidalea Rev Page Roberts 3ft
(28) Senecio White Diamond 2ft
(29) Gypsophila Bristol Fairy 4ft
(30) Rudbeckia subtomentosa 3ft
(31) Senecio przeewalskii 4ft
(32) Salva turkenstana superba 4ft
(33) Scabiosa caucasica Covent Garden 2½ft
(34) Aster Queen Mary 4ft
(35) Sidalcea oberon 2½ft
(36) Scabiosa ochroleuca 2ft
(37) Bocconia cordata 6ft
(38) Delphinium W. B. Cranfield
(39) Russel Lupins 4ft mixed
(40) Aster fillinpenudula Golden Plate 4ft
(41) Verbascum Cotswold Gem 4ft
(42) Solidago ballardi 5ft
(43) Veronica exaltata 4ft
(44) Salvia haematodes 4ft
(45) Sedalcia Sussex Beauty 3ft
(46) Verbascum hartleyi 4ft
(47) Thalictrum dipterocarpum 4ft
(48) Sidalcea Elsie Heugh 3½ft
(49) Solidago ballardi 5ft
(50) Helenuim Revcerton Gem 4ft
(51) Rudbeckia Golden Glow 5ft
(52) Astilbe davidii 4ft
(53) Lavetera albia rosea 5ft
(54) Aster Peace 4ft
(55) Veronica virginica 4ft
(56) Sidalcia Wensleydale 4ft
(57) Delphinium Lady Eleanor 6ft
(58) Scabiosa cancasica Miss Willmott 2ft
(59) Paeonia Mathew Celot 4ft

Normally, it is better to plant in the autumn, while the ground is still warm, than in the spring because this allows the roots to get established before the spring growing season. Conditions in your area, such as extremely dry or wet weather, could force you to plant in the spring. If you must plant at this time, you only lose a small amount of growth particularly if you take proper care to see that the young plants do not suffer from drought in the spring and early summer. This is the real danger of spring planting.

Planning

Be very careful in planning your border and lay it out as naturally as possible. Remember that not only are there tall flowers and dwarf ones, but there are early flowerers and late flowerers. If one part of the border is entirely planted with early-flowering varieties, it will look bare and derelict in late summer or autumn. Try, therefore, to have a late-flowering group of plants set in an earlier-flowering group to hide the gap once the early ones have been cut down. A border can be planted to look well every month from the spring to the first killing frost.

Obviously the dwarf plants should not be at the back of the border, nor the tall ones in front, but on the other hand do not arrange the border so that all the plants go up in 'steps'. It is good fun to allow some of the taller plants to come to the front of the border occasionally to break up any uniformity. The great thing is to aim for a natural look. Don't, for instance, have just one plant of one variety: have a group of them, three or four plants to form a drift—you get a better splash of colour and a less spotty effect. Don't set the plants in squares, triangles or circles; I have used the word drift on purpose, because the important thing is to have long-shaped groups, drifting as it were from one colour to another.

All kinds of borders can be planned: the all-blue border, the all-white border, the border with nothing but reds and pinks. But most people prefer a mixed border, and fortunately almost all plant colours mix quite well together. It is the foliage that seems to prevent that harsh clash sometimes seen in women's clothing, when they try to wear pinks, magentas and oranges at the same time!

Don't put the plants too close together. Look in the catalogue for the likely heights of the various plants. A delphinium that may grow say 6ft high may need 3ft on either side if it is to be seen in all its beauty and develop as it should. The plan on p 49 can be modified to suit any garden.

Mulching

The moment the planting has been completed, and the soil has been trodden down, a light raking should be given. The compost gardener then applies powdery compost or peat humus all over the border 1in deep. Thus the border will never have to be hoed—for no annual weed seeds will be able to grow. Further, the mulch will keep the moisture in the soil and the plants won't suffer in a dry summer. As elsewhere in the garden the worms may well pull some of the mulch into the soil, in so doing building up the humus content of the soil and improving soil structure; so a further dressing of compost will be given the following year to make up for what has disappeared. It depends of course on the condition of the soil. Where a garden has been neglected for years, or where quantities of chemical fertilisers have been used in the

Fine mixed vegetables. (*Harry Smith*)

Azaleas in a terraced London garden. (*Harry Smith*)

Apple – Bramley Seedling.
(*Harry Smith*)

Mulching with compost.
(*Harry Smith*)

past and no dung or compost added, then the humus content of the earth is bound to be low. If the worms pull in say half-an-inch, then another half-inch of compost or peat humus is added. After a few years, however, the worms will not pull in any more and the mulch stays as it is. Further, the border looks particularly attractive because of the pure brownness of the 'soil' in which the herbaceous plants grow.

Later care

Do not forget that some later care will benefit the look of your border. A clump of Michaelmas daisies or a clump of chrysanthemum maximum (ox-eye daisy), for instance, will never grow as well as they should unless the little growths (or 'spikes') they develop in the spring are thinned out. Thin out early and growth will develop, plus a gorgeous show. It is very important in the case of delphiniums to remove the unwanted stems as soon as they appear, for the longer you leave them on the plant the more they are robbing the roots.

Then, staking can easily make or mar a herbaceous border. If the plants are not staked they are apt to flop about all over the place, and if you overstake or stake badly the border looks a mass of bamboos and poles. The secret with most plants is to provide the supports early, and there is nothing like the 'twiggy' pea-stick for the plants that tend to spread, like Michaelmas daisies, heleniums, geums, phlox, etc. The pea-sticks are pushed into the ground among the plants before growth takes place in the spring, and as the stems grow they get the support they need while their foliage covers up the bareness of the sticks; thus the vital support is more or less invisible. The taller, stiffer types of plants, like delphiniums for instance, are best supported by bamboos or very thin stakes. These should be pushed into the ground behind the stems and the tying should not be too tight. It is generally necessary to have one bamboo to each tall stem and, in this case, it is possible to give each flower its correct spacing. Those who try and tie all the stems of a delphinium to one stake get a bunched-up effect which doesn't give the flowers a chance, and anyway looks hideous.

An old border

Sometimes a garden is taken over and there is a perennial herbaceous border already there. Perhaps it has grown too thick and overcrowded and needs renovation. This should be done preferably in the autumn or very early in the spring—the earlier the better. The plants should all be dug up and laid on old sacks, placed for the purpose on the lawn or path or whatever it may be. It is a good plan not to lift more plants than can be put back the same day. When the plants are out, whether just a small patch or the whole border, the soil should be forked over and plenty of fully composted powdery vegetable waste or peat humus added at two bucketsful to the square yard.

Into the same top 3in should be forked plant foods, such as bone meal at 3oz to the square yard, and wood ashes at 6oz to the square yard, plus a light dressing of hydrated lime applied on the surface if the soil tests have shown that this is necessary.

The top dressing of peat humus or, better still, home-made powdery brown compost is applied all over the soil an inch deep after replanting the border.

THE FLOWERING SHRUB BORDER

A shrub border can be very attractive and perhaps takes less time to keep in order than any other type of gardening; but let it be a coloured shrub border and not just one consisting of dreary evergreens!

Preparing and planting

Don't dig the land over to prepare the bed as is done normally; just dig out a hole the right size for each tree or shrub—it should be large enough to accommodate all the roots without cramping them. Spread the roots out evenly, not allowing them to be twisted or curled up. See that the center of the hole is slightly higher than the rest of the circumference. See that it is deep enough for the shrub to be planted about 1in lower than it was in the nursery where it came from. You ought to have no difficulty in finding the soil mark at the base of the stem.

Lilium, var Enchantment (*Harry Smith*)

As the holes are being filled in, see that the soil is trodden down firmly. Try and get the soil down fine, especially for the smaller shrubs—don't place big unbroken clods over the roots and expect them to re-root quickly. Tread the surface firmly, then rake it so as to prevent caking or puddling; but always leave the center of the hole slightly higher than the outside.

Move evergreens either in the early autumn or as soon as the ground can be worked in the spring, and if the weather is dry in the early summer syringe them over every day till they are established rather than watering them repeatedly. A screen of sacking placed round a shrub to give shade and ward off drying winds is a very effective way of keeping a rather tender specimen from drying after planting. Plant the non-evergreens in the autumn. If the garden soil is a heavy clay then spring planting is generally preferable to late autumn planting.

Choosing the shrubs

Don't forget to purchase the shrubs from a first-class nurseryman who specialises in them. Have them sent to you, preferably in 'cardboard' pots, when he recommends planting them in your locality. Remember, if you are buying berry-bearing shrubs whose flowers are uni-sexual, that is to say shrubs whose male and female flowers are borne on different plants, to order plants of both sexes, because the female plant will only bear berries when a male plant is nearby. A typical example of this is the holly.

It is possible to have shrubs flowering in almost every month of the year. The early flowerers include the forsythias, flowering currants, flowering cherries, almonds and witch hazels. In early summer there are the crab apples, brooms, lilacs, laburnum, spireas, azaleas, rhododendrons and ceanothus. In later summer come the escalonias, buddleias, mock orange (philadelphus) and cytisus nigrans. These are followed by the autumn-flowering shrubs, like the late-flowering types of clematis, the veronicas, the hibiscus and hosts of heaths, while even later than these come the winter-flowering shrubs such as lonicera fragantissima, yellow jasmine, viburnum fragrans, chimonathus fragrans and prunus subhirtella autumnalis.

In addition to shrubs that flower at different times, remember there are some that have coloured stems in winter; some with beautiful autumn colouring (there is a long list of these); some with handsome berries and fruits; some with lovely foliage. Then there are those which do best in particular positions or are tolerant of difficult conditions. Some will do quite well in a windy place; others like a poor soil. So discuss the position with the nurseryman. Describe to him the place where you want to put the shrub or tree; tell him whether the soil is heavy or light, acid or alkaline; say whether it is windswept or sunny. In fact, give the nurseryman all particulars you can so that you are likely to have the right tree or shrub in the right place.

Fruits of Pernettya mucronata alba (*Harry Smith*)

Pruning

The general rule for pruning flowering shrubs is to cut them back after flowering, especially those which flower on the shoots made during the previous summer. Shrubs that bear their blooms on the current year's wood may be cut back quite hard any time during the shrub's dormant period. Evergreen shrubs are best pruned in April. Always prune with a good pair of secateurs or a sharp knife, making a clean cut. Prune to keep the shrub within measurable limits and a good shape, and to let in light and air to enable the mature bearing wood to ripen properly.

Mulching

After planting the shrubs properly cover the soil in the bed with well-rotted compost, or—if you haven't got this—peat humus. Remember to put this 1in deep all over the bed, please. It will act as a mulch and keep the moisture in below, as well as preventing the annual weeds from growing.

Feed the shrubs with a fish manure containing 6–7 per cent potash. Apply this at 3–4oz to the square yard in the winter each year and again in the summer if the shrubs are not growing strongly enough.

Varieties

Good varieties for growing on the compost system include:

Barberis aquifolium	— See Mahonia below
,, darwinii	— dark green glossy leaves, orange flowers, purple berries
,, stenophylla	— glossy leaves, yellow flowers
,, verruculosa	— small glossy leaves, pendulous yellow flowers, purple fruits
Buddleia globosa	— ball-like orange flowers in May, June, semi-evergreen
,, davidii	— mauve flowers, July, August
Choisya ternata	— glossy leaves, white blossoms, fragrant
Cotoneaster microphyllus	— glossy leaves, red berries, 2ft
,, franchetti	— grey-green foliage, semi-evergreen, orange-scarlet berries
Deutzia gracilis rosea	— pink flowers, 4ft
Escallonia C. F. Ball	— large crimson flowers
,, Pride of Donard	— bright red flowers, June
Forsythia intermedia Beatrix Farrand	— large yellow flowers
,, ,, Lynwood	— golden-yellow flowers
Hydrangea hortensis	— red and pink for limy soils, and blue forms for acid soils
,, sargentiana	— blue and white flowers, likes shade
Hypericum calycinum	— grows in shade, golden flowers, dwarf smothery
Lilac (Syringa) Charles Joly	— rich purple-red
,, ,, General Pershing	— violet-purple
,, ,, Souvenir de Louis Spath	— deep purple, highly scented
Mahonia aquifolium	— grows under trees, holly-like leaves, golden-yellow flowers, 4ft

Pernettya mucronata	— dislikes lime, evergreen, lovely red-pink berries, 4ft
Philadelphus Avalanche	— sun or shade, white highly scented flowers, 5ft
,, Manteau D'Hermine	— creamy-white scented flowers, 5ft
Potentialla fruticosa Katherine Dykes	— sulphur-yellow, flowers all summer, 4ft
,, ,, Tangerine	— golden flowers, flushed orange, 2ft
Pyracantha cocinea orange glow	— orange berries, sun or shade, 10ft
Senecio greyii	— silver-grey leaves, yellow daisy flowers, sunny spot, 3ft
Skimmia japonica	— evergreen, white scented flower, red berries, 4ft
Spartium jupceum	— emerald-green leaves gold-yellow pea-like flowers—poor soil, 8ft
Symphorocarpus Magic Berry	— compact, pink berries, 5ft
Veronica (Syn. Hebe) buxifolia	— evergreen, bright green leaves, white flowers, 3ft
,, highdownensis	— narrow green leaves, blue flowers, 3ft
,, pimeleoides minor	— grey-blue foliage, mauve-blue flowers, 12in
,, traverversi	— evergreen small-leaved white-flowered, good in town gardens, 4ft
Viburnum Carlesii	— hardy, pink buds, fragrant white flowers, 5ft
,, fragrans	— highly scented white flowers, winter-flowering, 6ft
,, opulus sterile	— round balls of white, flowers in June, 7ft
,, tinus	— winter-flowering evergreen, pink buds and white flowers, likes shade, 7ft
Weigela (Syn. Diervilla) Bristol Ruby	— showy ruby-red flowers, 6ft
,, florida folius purpereus	— pink flowers, purple foliage, 3ft
,, Newport Red	— red flowers, orange marks—likes sheltered spot, 6ft

These varieties grow well in a temperate climate with mild winters. Some are hardy enough to survive more severe winters or if not there are species which have been bred to withstand extremes of temperature. Consult your local nurseries for information about your area before deciding on your plantings.

ROSES

The rose is found almost everywhere. It produces its blooms without any difficulty in the gardens of smoky towns as well as in the countryside. It's best when massed and so it is always worth while giving up a portion of the garden to a bed where roses and only roses can be planted. The larger gardens will of course have a number of beds, but they will keep the varieties of the same colour growing separately in a bed of their own. It isn't quite so much the size of the bed that counts as the massed effect.

There are all types of roses: bushes, standards, pot roses, ramblers, climbers, weeping standards and so on; the beginner need not worry too much about the sub-divisions. More HTs (hybrid teas) and floribundas are grown today than any other type. The glorious oranges and bronzes have arrived as the result of the marriage between the pernettianas and HTs. The wichurianas are the rambler roses, while the climbing roses are really HTs that have been 'transformed' and 'forced' to adopt a climbing habit.

Preparing and planting

Don't worry if you haven't got what the gardener calls the 'right' soil; most soils will grow roses. Fork the ground over very lightly just to level it. Do the forking as early as possible to allow the soil to settle before planting. Rake into the top 2in meat and bone meal or fish manure at 4 to 5oz per square yard, and if the acidity test shows it to be necessary (see p 39) give the surface a dusting with hydrated lime at 6oz to the square yard.

Having planted firmly and left the soil level, apply the organic matter (either a compost substitute, or the powdery compost made in the garden compost bins) all over the bed to the depth of 1in; thus no annual weeds will grow. Further, because no hoeing will be done the roots of the roses will not be disturbed. Roses grow far better with this compost system and there is far less trouble from mildew and no trouble from black spot: the spores of this disease blow up from the soil on to the leaves of the roses, and when there is a barrier of organic matter on the soil this upward movement is prevented.

When the bushes arrive examine them and if any of the roots have been damaged cut them back with a sharp knife. If they have been on a long journey put them in a bucket of water for two or three hours so that they get a good soaking. Do not plant in frosty weather. Dig a hole sufficiently large for the roots to be spread out evenly and deep enough for the union of bud and stock to be buried. Cover the roots with soil that has been broken up well and tread down. Don't be afraid of firming really well because firm planting is essential.

Always try and plant in the autumn because then new roots will be sent out before the winter sets in. When planting ramblers or climbers next to a wall or fence, make the hole 1ft away so that the roots have a chance of growing properly.

Plant bush roses, whether HTs or floribundas, 20in apart and the dwarfer floribundas 18in apart.

Composting the rose bed

Pruning

Remember that the main idea behind pruning is to try (a) to limit the number of branches and (b) to produce roses of first-class quality only. In the winter, dead or diseased wood or crossing and misplaced branches should be cut out completely. In the spring, just before active growth begins, the main pruning of the HTs and floribundas is done, and this consists of cutting back the one-year-old growth to within three good eyes of their base. Use a sharp knife or a pair of good secateurs and make the cut just above a bud at an angle of 45°.

On climbing roses the dead wood should be thinned out, and as the base of the plant tends to become bare after a time, cut back one or two of the older shoots in the early spring to within four buds or 'eyes' of their base so that new growth will fill in the bare portion of the plant. After flowering, in the summer, thin out the growths over two years of age to prevent the plants from becoming overcrowded.

On ramblers, cut out the old wood (this is the wood that has flowered) a few weeks after flowering, and tie up the young growths in their place. With weeping standards, shorten the long shoots that trail on to the ground, and remove the older shoots as near to the head as possible; but if there are not enough new shoots, leave some of the older ones.

General regular work

Every year there is a certain amount of regular routine work to be done—though not of course hoeing if you have used that organic mulch. For instance, though you may have pruned carefully just above a bud in the spring, this bud may go blind. As a result it may be necessary, after growth has started, to cut back the growth still further, ie to just above a growing bud that is not blind. Then early in May it is quite a good plan to go over the bushes and rub out with the thumb and forefinger any young growths that look as if they are going to overcrowd the centre of the tree.

If larger and better blooms are required, disbudding should be carried out. At the ends of the growths will be found a terminal bud and two or three side buds, and it is these side flower buds that should be removed, when they are young, the central bud being retained. Remember to cut back all the suckers that grow up from the roots: these are the wild growths that have a quite different appearance from the rest of the bush. A sucker usually has more thorns on it than the true rose, and leaves are usually smaller and more numerous.

Summer prune after the first blooming in June by pruning back the end of the growths—by, say, 7in. The result is that second blooms appear in the autumn. Though the rose will withstand prolonged droughts it is sometimes necessary, in very dry seasons, to give a thorough soaking. This means putting the hose (with one of those whirling sprinklers attached) into position for at least half an hour.

In the spring if red spiders or aphides attack severely, spray with liquid derris or rotenone, and if there is any sign of a fungus disease, use captan to control black spot and karathane for mildew (see Chapter 12); but when growing roses the compost way there is seldom any trouble from fungus diseases.

Don't forget to feed, adding plant foods every year. Fish manure is excellent and may be used at 3 to 4oz per square yard every spring. Rake up all the fallen leaves in autumn and place them on the compost heap to rot down. With some diseases, particularly black spot, the spores are carried over on these leaves from year to year—but not if they are properly composted.

Those who live in towns may have to replant rose bushes every nine or ten years, but it helps matters considerably if the dressings of hydrated lime are given—at, say, 5oz to the square yard; for town smoke brings about soil acidity. Town dwellers are advised not to grow delicate shades of creams, ivories, and lemons, but to stick to reds, deep pinks and salmons. Syringing over the bushes with clear water once a week in the evenings is very helpful, for it washes off the soot deposits.

Varieties

To give a complete list of roses and their varieties would be impossible in a book of this size. Here, therefore, are brief selections of the various roses, under their headings, with a word or two of description.

Hybrid tea roses

Crimson Glory	— velvety crimson, fragrant
Grandmère Jenny	— peach-pink on yellow, scented
Grandpa Dickson	— yellow, vigorous, immense blooms
Lady Sylvia	— rose-salmon pink, scented
Mrs Sam McGredy	— coppery-orange, flushed red
Piccadilly	— bright scarlet, golden reverse, an excellent bi-colour
Shiralee	— saffron-yellow, flushed marigold, disease-resistant
Shot Silk	— cherry-cerise, overshot salmon, mildew-resistant, fragrant
Super Star	— vermilion, fragrant
Wendy Cussons	— rose-red, damask fragrance

Floribunda roses

Antique	— scarlet gold, bright and warming
Early Bird	— rose-opal, puts up with bad weather
Paint Box	— multi-coloured
Princess Michiko	— orange and gold, bright
Trio	— gold and red, brightens any dark corner
Sea Pearl	— pearly-pink, dark-green foliage
Summer Song	— orange and lemon, robust, low-growing

Hybrid teas on the whole produce the more beautiful, double, scented roses which are at their best, say, in June and September. Floribundas generally produce masses of roses on a stem and go on flowering month after month.

7

THE VEGETABLE GARDEN

THE main difference between compost vegetable growing and the normal old-fashioned vegetable culture is, of course, that no digging is done in preparation—unless in the case of celery, where a shallow trench is prepared. Even here, however, green celery or the self-blanching celery may be grown without.

The plan is to make plenty of compost and, when it is fully ripe and in a brown powdery form, to put it all over the plot to be used for vegetables, to a depth of at least half-an-inch. Some gardeners have complained that they cannot make enough compost from material obtained from the home and garden, but such men and women forget to compost their newspapers and magazines, and maybe they do not make the effort to obtain organic waste from their local supermarket which they might let you collect. If you happen to be a very good friend of the manager, plastic bags can be given to the market and collected once or twice a week when full. It is more likely that you will have to do the filling yourself. This sounds like work—and it is—but it does ensure (a) that the very valuable vegetable matter is not wasted by being burnt or buried in the local dump and (b) that you have ample cheap composting matter which will soon build up the humus content of your soil.

However, I have digressed, but deliberately so! Once the compost is in position, say in the autumn before frost, the vegetable area can be left alone for the winter. The worms will get to work while the ground is not frozen and will pull some of the compost in and do the necessary aeration, as described in Chapter 1. After three or four years of this treatment there will be in the region of 6,000,000 worms per acre. They will chew up the soil and the compost you have added and produce wormcasts rich in plant foods below the soil level.

When spring time comes the compost layer—or what is left of it—will be lightly rototilled into the soil. For those who have no mechanical rototiller (see p 24) a light shallow forking will do, the idea being to prepare the surface to the depth of an inch or so. When this method of vegetable culture has been carried out for five or six years it will be discovered that the top 4 or 5in have a high organic content, rich in humus; this depth of soil is almost pure 'terreau', as the French call it. The roots of most of the crops will concentrate themselves in this region. In addition there should be hardly any annual weeds to control in the summer the weed seeds have been killed in the compost and so hoeing is reduced to a minimum—say a scuffling here and there four or five times in the whole season.

The second effect of gardening organically is that the pest and disease problem is reduced to a minimum also: no bean beetle, no blackfly on broad beans, no aphides on brassicas, no carrot rust fly on carrots, no onion fly or thrips on onions and so on. In dry periods when cauliflower causes so much trouble, the organically grown plants crop heavily.

Incidentally, at Arkley Manor, we have ceased to thin our carrots and beets; we sow thinly of course, but the plants are allowed to come up naturally and we leave them. Though they are growing cheek by jowl and don't seem to have enough room, the roots are large enough and, of course, very delicious. The whole question of taste comes into this method of growing, because the flavour of the salads, tomatoes, peas, beans, brussels sprouts and even cabbage is 'out of this world'. The good old-fashioned flavour that our grandmother is reputed to have known has come back now that the land is free from chemicals, and now that the millions of living organisms in the soil can do their work in an unrestricted manner.

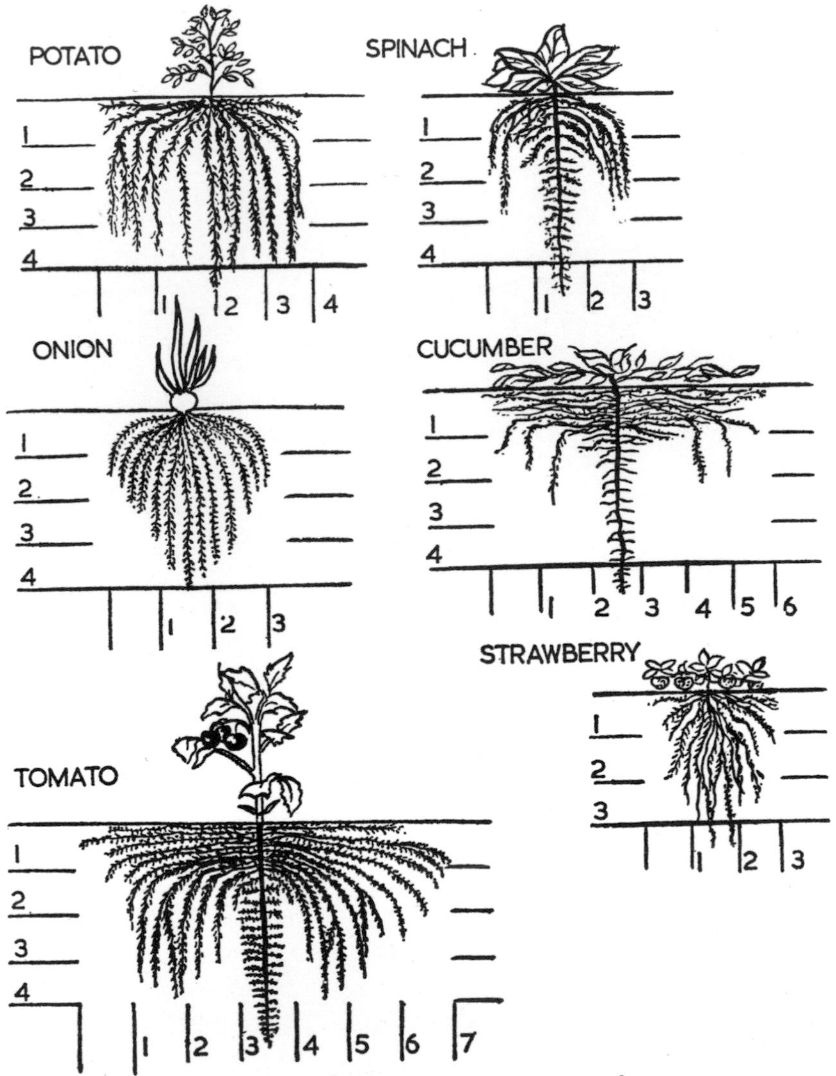

How vegetable roots need to spread

Seed sowing

The land has been prepared in the natural way, and now comes the sowing of the seed. When the right time comes (see the chart), tread the strip where the row of vegetables is to grow to firm it and then rake it level. Put down a line from one end of the plot to the other—and peg it down tight. Using a draw hoe with its longest edge against the line, scratch out a drill 2in deep for the bigger seeds like peas and beans, and only 1in deep for the smaller seeds. In the V-shaped drill sprinkle the seeds as thinly as you can. In fact in the case of the peas and beans you can space them out 2 or 3in apart. Rake over the land again to bury the seeds and, by

'Aristocrat', a tall, typically heavy-cropping brussels sprout

holding the rake handle perpendicularly, firm the row with the rake head. Then give another light raking to remove the rake-head marks.

Although years ago I carefully measured the exact distances needed between the rows of each vegetable, and would always advise beets at, say, 15in apart, and lettuce at 12in apart, today I find that 18in apart suits all the plants except the larger ones like brussels sprouts, for which the rows are double-spaced, ie 3ft apart. This makes it easier for the rototilling machine to work down in between the rows and so do mechanically what hoeing has to be done.

Take the trouble to buy good, properly harvested and well-prepared seed. Always insist on the best varieties: by best, I mean varieties that will suit you as regards height, size and flavour, as well as the types which will mature during your growing season and are appropriate for your climate. To buy cheap seed at any old store is foolish.

INDIVIDUAL VEGETABLES

Asparagus

This is all the more popular now that amateur gardeners are finding it easy to grow on compost lines. It is a crop that prefers a sandy soil or a sandy loam—but with plenty of properly made compost it can be grown well in clays. When the crop is coming through the ground some protection should be given to the bed from cold winds, for they will twist and malform the stalks.

Use clean land, eliminating the perennial weeds first. Don't raise your own plants, but always buy rust-resistant crowns of either one of the new hybrids or the old standby such as Martha Washington or KBF. These should be one-year-old crowns, which transplant far better than two- or three-year-olds.

Prepare the soil by using a rototiller, and if a machine for the purpose is not available, carry out a light forking 6in deep, adding at the same time powdery compost at 4 bucketsful to the square yard or one of the substitutes instead. Give also a seaweed or fish fertiliser at 4oz to the square yard.

Do the actual planting in the early spring, aiming to set the plants 6in deep and 2½ft apart in the rows. The next row should be 4ft away. Spread the roots out like rays of the sun when planting them in a 6in wide trench and cover them with 3in of good soil mixed with compost on a 50–50 basis. As the plants grow in the summer, more soil and compost will be hoed over them until at last the soil is 'live'.

Mulch the soil alongside the rows, and in fact all over the area occupied by the asparagus, with 1in of powdery compost or peat humus. This will make hoeing unnecessary all the summer.

Don't attempt to eat any asparagus until the third year after planting. (That's the rub!) That year it will help if another layer of compost or substitute can be applied, making the depth over the bed about 4in. Cut when the asparagus is seen well above the compost, using a narrow knife and making the cut 4in below soil level. It may be necessary to harvest every day during the season, especially as asparagus tastes best when cooked and served within two hours of cutting. Cease cutting after five or six weeks, thus allowing the plants to build up their strength for another year. At the end of the season, when the fern is turning brown, cut it down to soil level and compost it.

Beans

Concentrate on a stringless *French* bean like Processor, and pick it on the young side.

Runner beans can be grown on the same spot year after year, so you can have a permanent structure for them to climb. There is no need to dig a trench for them as some people advise. Remember that beans are really perennials, so if you plant in a sheltered spot they will come up every year, especially when the site is covered with an inch of compost.

Sow *broad* beans successionally, with three or four weeks between sowing; try a sowing in early November and a second sowing in April. Young broad beans can be eaten raw.

Beets

Sow fairly thinly. Harvest first of all when golf-ball size and serve hot. Leave other roots to get larger for salads. To stretch out the harvest cover the beets with a deep mulch of hay after the first few frosts and harvest them as you need them into winter. With a tall marking stake you can dig them through snow.

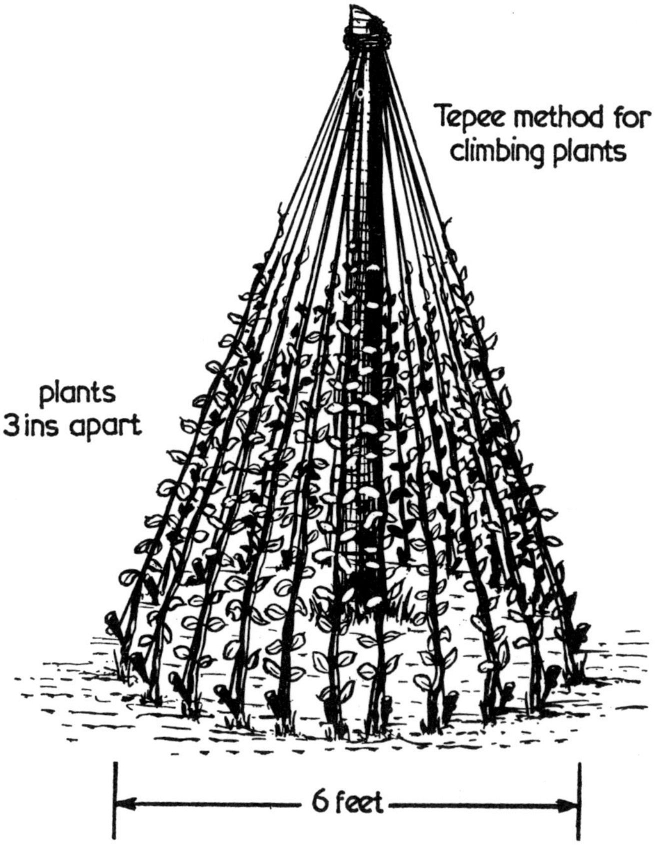

'Tepee' method for growing runner or pole beans

Broccoli (Sprouting broccoli)

Set out plants in the early spring. They can stand some frost. If you plant seed at the same time you might get a late crop in the fall. When harvesting, first cut out the central flower-head which will be large. This stimulates smaller shoots to form heads which develop over the next months. Try Green Comet or Di Cicco.

Brussels sprouts

These grow well in a cool climate. Sow as for broccoli. The individual sprouts grow on a central stalk and are best picked after the first frost.

Cabbage

For spring cabbage sow on about 15 July, planting out on 15 September, or sow on 15 August in situ and thin out. Remember there are spring cabbages to use in the spring! These are very useful and delicious. Summer cabbages can be had from spring sowings and so can winter cabbages. Thus it isn't very difficult to have compost-grown cabbages all the year round. I do. Three good varieties are Unwins Foremost for the spring, Fillgap for the summer, and Christmas Drumhead for winter.

Carrots

Sow one or two rows as soon as the ground can be worked in the spring and, if you like them, one or more rows about a month later. Don't bother to thin—pull the roots as and when they are large enough and you need them. They come up easily in compost-mulched soil.

Onions, about three-quarter grown, on undug, composted ground

Cauliflower

These are much more difficult to grow than cabbages but they revel in compost culture. The plants insist on the minimum of disturbance. You can dibble cabbages in—but cauliflowers like to be transplated with a good ball of soil around the roots and then an inch of compost put around them. Planting cannot be done until the soil is warm. Cauliflowers must never stop growing, once in the ground, so water is necessary. For pure white heads you must tie the leaves over them when they appear. You can avoid this chore by planting one of the purple-headed varieties.

Celery

Grow a self-blanching variety, because it doesn't need earthing up. The stems are neat, crisp and stringless. Sow the seed in boxes containing a seed-starting medium in the greenhouse in March; transplant the seedlings to a frame, if you have one, setting them 3in apart, in early April. Plant in land very liberally treated with compost, placing the plants 8in apart in rows, with 24in between the rows.

Lettuces

Grow three different varieties: 1, a butterhead like Suzan or Bibb, 2, a crisp, curly-leaf type like Wonderful or Salad-bowl; and 3, a delicious sweet baby cos called Sugar Cos. It pays to make a number of small sowings in order to get succession, say one-quarter of a row at a time. Sow thinly and shallowly, and then when the seedlings are through, thin to 9in apart. Be prepared to water well if the weather is dry. Sow again when the previous sowing shows through.

Marrows

Useful to grow in an odd spot, especially on an odd heap of compost if available. Pinch the ends of the young shoots when they are 3ft long, to encourage the production of side growths. The alternative is to grow bush marrows and especially Early Gem. Grow zuccini because they can be eaten whole—or, of course, the courgette.

Onions

The easiest way of growing good onions in a compost garden is to plant onion 'sets', little onion bulbs specially grown for the purpose. Plant these out at the end of March in rows 12in apart, allowing 6in between the sets. Just push the bulbs into heavily composted soil so that they are buried half-way. Then let them grow without any further attention other than keeping down the weeds. Harvest the large well-ripened onions early in September.

Parsley

You can sow this on either side of onions or carrots, if you have in the past had trouble with maggots in the roots: it does seem to keep away the flies that lay their eggs on the rows of crops. It makes a good edging plant for the vegetable plot.

Parsnips

Sow the seed early in the spring at about the same time you sow carrots. The seed tends to blow in the wind so choose a calm day. Sow lettuce seed in the same drill and these will mark the row early. Thin out the parsnips to 8in apart, leaving a lettuce between each root and its neighbour, and you will thus get an inter-crop.

Peas

Compost-grown peas are particularly delicious. Sow the seed in March in drills 1in deep and 18in to 2ft apart depending on the height of the variety. (To save time and sticks, grow the dwarfer types.) Try the Sugar Peas, which you eat pod and all, or Heston Mini which grows only 12in high and will usually live through the winter if sown in October. Recette is a triple-podded maincrop—ie having three pods on every stem. The peas are light green and taste like 'petit pois', very sweet. If you have a deep freeze, grow Victory Freezer, a 2½ft pea which bears pods in pairs of superb quality.

Mangetout peas—pods are eaten as well as peas (*E. H. Greenwood*)

Potatoes

Find out locally which variety grows best in your area and plant certified disease-free seed potatoes by getting out a V-shaped drill about 4in deep and lay sections of tuber containing one eye about 12in apart in this. Put ½in of compost or substitute along the drill and then cover with mulch hay or lawn clippings. There is no need to put any earth on the row, making harvesting free from digging.

Apple – Charles Ross.
(*Harry Smith*)

Summer borders.
(*Harry Smith*)

Woodland garden.
(*Harry Smith*)

Small but thriving garden.
(*Harry Smith*)

Spinach

This is particularly good in a compost garden and doesn't go to seed quickly. Grow successional pickings by successional sowings, sowing a quarter of a row every three weeks, as with lettuce. Don't forget the value of New Zealand spinach which does not bolt during hot weather. Spinach is as good eaten raw as cooked.

Swedes

These should be grown as turnips. The big farm swedes are far better than the garden swedes and are just as easy to grow, although they are liable to club-root disease. Try growing Tipperary or Field Purple Top.

Sweet Corn

Sweet corn takes up quite a bit of space but the only way to have really fresh corn on the cob is to grow it yourself. Plant the corn about two weeks after your last expected severe frost in hills or rows depending on your whim, but making sure that the plants grow in close proximity rather than spread out in a long row. Space the plants 1ft apart in rows 3ft apart or 3 to 4 plants in hills 3ft apart. To spread out your harvest either plant early and late varieties or plant plots out at one-week intervals. Sweet corn uses plenty of nourishment so you might add some fish manure to your compost during your first few years of culture; afterwards the compost will make the soil so rich you no longer need supplements. In Britain, you will not succeed with this crop in a cool, wet summer.

Tomatoes

Tomatoes grow prolifically on compost. You must either start the plants indoors during March or April or buy the plants from a nursery. Choose plants that are resistant to verticillium or fusarium wilts if these are a problem. If your space is limited you will need to stake the plants, otherwise let them spread out over the compost-covered earth, planting them about 30in apart. You can choose from many varieties and find that they taste better than purchased ones.

Turnips

An excellent summer vegetable if grown quickly, which is exactly what can be done in a compost garden. They can also be a useful winter vegetable.

Winter-storage turnips are members of the cabbage family called swedes. These should be grown as turnips, using wood ash to combat club-root disease by covering the drill with ash when the plants get their second leaves. If club-root is a problem try a resistant variety.

Outdoor tomatoes at Arkley, grown under cloches in early stages
(*Pat Thomas*)

Unusual vegetables

Those we grow well in the Experimental Gardens at Arkley Manor include the Blue Coco runner bean, with its blue pods; the celeriac, which produces a round root like a turnip but tasting of celery heart; salsify, a white root just as easy to grow as carrots, but with an 'oystery' flavour; kohlrabi, another root crop which must be eaten when the roots are the size of tennis balls.

Endive is as easy to grow as lettuce, only you must cover the plants up when fully grown, with a large pot or box to blanch them—to turn the leaves white, so that they will be crisp and not bitter.

8

THE FRUIT GARDEN

THOSE who love flavour, those who want heavier crops, those who crave for freedom from disease in the fruit garden, gain one extra advantage from growing the compost way: it is the no-root-disturbance way. This is the basis of the culture. No forking or hoeing must be done while the trees or bushes or canes are growing. The apples, pears, plums and peaches will be grown in grass, the soft fruit such as gooseberries, red currants, black currants, raspberries, blackberries and blueberries in a mat of straw 1ft deep and the strawberries in soil covered with compost 1in deep.

TOP FRUIT

Cordons

If the garden is small the best way to grow the apples and pears is as cordons. These are single-stemmed trees trained at an angle of 45° on a post and wire contraption. The posts are put in 6ft apart and 6ft high and wires should be stretched in between, starting at 3ft high from the soil and after that 2ft apart. The cordons are tied to these with thick soft twine.

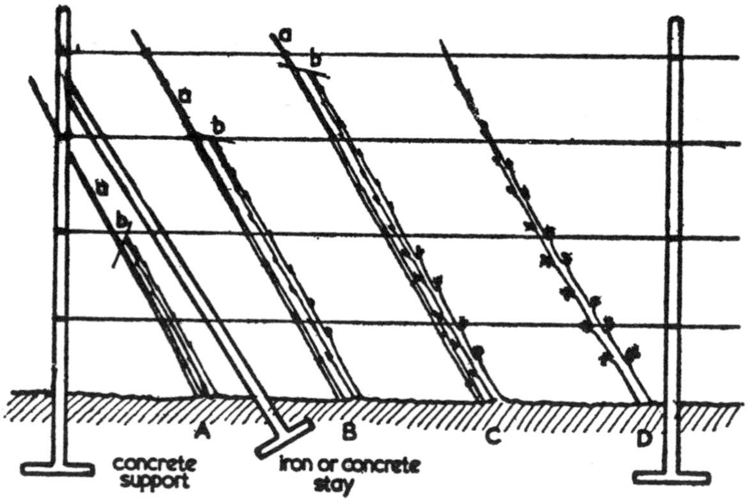

Training single cordons

The apples and pears under this system are planted 2ft apart and the laterals, or side growths, are pruned back each year to within 1in of their base. These cordons may be planted against a wall or fence where they will take up little room. Here they will have to be mulched with compost 1in deep and a foot wide at their base. In the garden proper they may be at the edge of, say, the lawn—so they are growing in grass.

Bush or dwarf trees

In any part of the garden a well-housed bush or dwarf apple or pear—or even plum for that matter—looks very attractive when in flower and beautiful when covered with delicious fruits in the summer and autumn. Plant the trees well apart, say 10 to 12ft, and give them room to grow. This also gives room for you to use the rotary mower in between the trees. Don't leave a ring of dug soil around each tree as some people do; the grass can grow right up to the stem, where you have to cut it by hand. Feed with well-rotted compost in the autumn at three bucketsful to the square yard.

Plant the trees shallow, so as not to bury the union of the stock and scion (the part where the grafting was done in the nursery). Plant firmly, however, and stake each tree properly, tying it to the stake with a plastic tie. This is a special strap which does not injure the bark of the tree or harbour insect pests.

There are dwarf peaches available since 1971, and these are grafted like the apples and pears on to dwarfing stocks. (The stock is the root part of the tree.) Ask for the apples that you buy to be supplied on Type 1X stocks and the pears on Type Quince C stocks. If you have very sandy soil and wish to grow weak-growing varieties so that the trees do not grow too top-heavy and suffer in gales, then the trees can be on Type X11 stocks. Before buying the trees consult your local nurseries about the best trees and root stocks for your area.

Grass cutting

When growing the trees in grass (and they are best grown in grass) be sure to keep the sward cut short. This means cutting nine or ten times during the season with no grass-box—the whole idea being to allow the grass clippings to return to the soil where they will rot and the worms will pull them in.

In addition to this it will be necessary to give some extra organic matter such as powdery compost, peat humus, rotted manure, spoiled hay, coffee grounds, etc, all at about 2 bucketsful to the square yard.

Pruning

The cordons will be pruned in the summer. Directly the side shoots reach a length of 9in they will be cut back to within an $\frac{1}{8}$in of their base. This means look over the trees once every month and the moment any shoot has reached the 9in length it will be pruned.

Dwarf trees, when established, can be pruned in a similar manner, but until the bushes are formed into, say, a goblet shape, the pruning consists of cutting back the one-year-old end growths or leads by about half, to just above a bud pointing outwards. Laterals or side growths may either be pruned back by three-quarters or may (if in the right place) be treated as leaders so as to form new branches. Remember pruning does not produce fruit, but it does ensure that it is produced where you want it. The less you prune the more fruit you will get and the sooner you will get it—but you want to have a nice-looking tree.

Varieties

Apples: Dessert varieties are, of course, delicious for eating raw and most of them are also delicious cooked. They are particularly good when compost-grown.

Merton Worcester	— nice early crimson apple
Laxton's Fortune	— beautiful red mid-season variety
Tydeman's Early	— delicious early kind

The following cooking apples are also recommended:

The Queen	— bakes like a snowball; beautifully fluffy

The apple orchard at Arkley (*author*)

Early Victoria	— very early and deliciously frothy when cooked
Lord Derby	— the best for mince pies
Bramley Seedling	— delicious for pies; but very strong grower and too large for small gardens
Thomas Rivers	— juicy and very fragrant
Charles Ross	— large eater, October–November, beautiful colour—yellow and red
Egremont Russet	— true russet, crisp and tasty; grows upright; late
Idared	— moderately vigorous; pale greenish-yellow fruit with bright red flush
Queen Cox	— brilliant crimson Cox's Orange Pippin; late

Pears: Grow these also by growing in grass and feeding with compost once a year in January —3 bucketsful to the square yard.

Doyenné du Comice	— the most delicious pear I know; late. Must have a pollinator
Glou Morceau	— grown as a pollinator for Doyenné du Comice
Conference	— easiest of the pears to grow; mid-season
William	— delicious pear most people know; early

Peaches

Bonanza	— new dwarf bush peach that only saw the light of day in 1970

Plums

Victoria	— lovely eater or cooker

SOFT FRUITS

Buy really good virus-free bushes in the case of the soft fruits. Put in your order early, say in the summer, and aim to take delivery of the soft fruits concerned in November. It is always as well to do the planting before the soil gets cold in the winter. Standardise the rows—have them 6ft apart, but the canes should be 2ft apart in the rows. After planting cut down the black currant bushes and the raspberry canes to within 6in of soil level; the red currant bushes may be left as they are, because they bear on the old wood.

The moment the planting and pruning has been completed (and note there has been no special preparation of the plot first of all, no digging and no forking), the area should be covered with straw 1ft deep. Any old straw will do. Over the straw will be sprinkled a good fish manure with 100 per cent potash, at 3oz to the square yard. Allow the organic food to be washed in gradually by the rain. Each July, after picking the fruit, give a similar dose. If the worms pull in a good deal of the straw a top dressing will have to be given from time to time, but it is seldom, if ever, necessary to have to add any more straw after the first four years.

The lawn method

There may be some who dislike the use of straw, though with me it gives excellent results. The alternative is to grow the canes or bushes in grass—ie, a lawn. Dig holes for the planting, put the grass sods back, and firm. Then keep the grass mown close all the summer and feed with organic fertiliser as in the case of the straw-covered plot. At the end of four years it will be necessary to apply some more organic matter, such as compost, spent hops, coffee grounds, poultry manure with peat, seaweed, and so on at 3 large bucketsful per square yard. The idea is to add more humus-forming material than the grass mowings are able to give.

Varieties

These grow particularly well in straw or in grass, ie compost-wise.

Gooseberries	
Careless	— mid-season; large, pale green
Pixwell	— green berry; upright grower, highly resistant to mildew
Golden Drop	— yellow, of excellent flavour
Crown Bob	— late; red, oval
Black currants	
Amos Black	— late; fine berry of good flavour
Mendip Cross	— early; large berries
Wellington XXX	— mid-season; fine flavour; good grower
Red currants & White currants	
Rondom	— the largest red currant
Laxton's No 1	— heavy cropper; berries have thin skin
White Grape	— large sweet white currant
Raspberries	
Malling Jewel	— resistant to disease; superb fruit
Malling Exploit	— early heavy cropper; large berries
Norfolk Giant	— late; fruit often lasts till the autumn

Strawberries

These, growing on the ground as they do, are best mulched with compost 1in deep. It is a simple matter to plant the one-year-old specimens in August or early September. This early planting makes all the difference to the cropping year after year for the four years the bed will be down.

Plant firmly, spreading the roots up. See that the base of the plant sits on the top of the soil. After planting at 2ft apart between the rows and 18in apart in the rows—cover the soil with compost 1in deep. This will not only smother the annual weed seeds and prevent them from growing but provide a mulch and so preserve the moisture in the soil. When the strawberries appear they are kept beautifully clean by ripening on the warm compost. Further, slugs will not attack the berries because they dislike 'walking' on the compost—they keep away. Apply more compost in a year's time, 'top up'. There will be no hoeing to do and the strawberries will love this as they have no root disturbance; thus they grow large and crop very heavily indeed.

Leave the strawberry bed down for three or four years, but each year plant up a few more rows so that you will have succession. Runners will form on the plants in July and August: select the best of these and plant them out in August in rows where you want them to grow. Then, having made your choice, cut off all the other runners on the plants and put them on the compost heap.

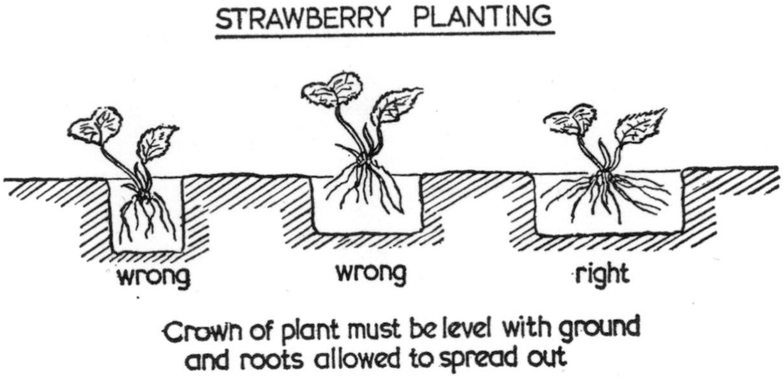

Strawberry planting

Varieties

Crusader	— clear red; superb flavour; early
Royal Sovereign	— Shewell-Mardett strain; mid-season; excellent flavour
Templar	— late; vigorous grower; heavy cropper
Cambridge Favourite	— early; fruit of good shape; resistant to mildew

Climbing cane fruits

If you have a fence you want to cover, or any old shed—or even if you don't mind putting up a strip of wire netting especially for the purpose—then you can plant some blackberries, loganberries, and hybrid berries. They need to have about 12ft of room each so that they can spread. Much of the old wood must be cut out each winter and the new young wood tied up in its place. After planting cover the soil with compost 1in deep so there will be no hoeing to do. The mulch will also keep the moisture in the soil.

Large, heavy cropping strawberry plants, grown on the compost system and never hoed

Good varieties to grow are:

Blackberries

Bedford Giant	— early August
Oregon Thornless	— early September; excellent flavour

Loganberries

LY, 59 Clone	— vigorous; hardy; prolific
Thornless Loganberry	— lovely thornless strong-growing cane

Hybrid berries

Malling Hybrid 53–16	— purple fruit; makes marvellous jam; few seeds

Giant pumpkin (*Harry Smith*)

9

THE LAWNS

PROBABLY there is no good garden anywhere without a lawn of some kind. The lawn may be largish or it may be quite a small sward on which folk sit to have their tea. There are lawns in the front with beds in them gay with flowers; there are lawns at the back formed largely as a surround for large rose-beds; there are lawns that cover rolling banks, and lawns that seem to go off in the distance forming the vista which gives such a rest to the eye.

I am afraid that England's climate promotes much better lawn growth than that in most parts of America. You will get beautiful and healthy grass by using the compost method, but the results will be tempered by your climate. Don't become a slave to your lawn; give it the attention it needs but don't try to create a golf green for you will probably never have time to use it.

TURF OR SEED

A lawn can either be made from sowing seed or from laying turf. The turf method gives quicker results but is much more expensive and it is difficult today to get a really good turf; too often you see advertised in the local paper and it is just some rough pasture that has been skimmed off any old field. Most of the finest lawns I have seen were grown from seed. My advice, therefore, is to concentrate on the preparation of the soil and the sowing of the seed.

PREPARING THE GROUND

Don't spend too much time on levelling unless you want to use the lawn for playing certain games. If the lawn has a slight slope, leave it as a slight slope and just concentrate on making the actual surface even, and filling up the holes and depressions.

On the other hand, if you really are keen on a perfect level, you can achieve it with a spirit level, a quantity of pegs and a piece of wood 10ft long, 6in wide and 2in broad. Dip the pegs in white paint to a depth of 6in, and leave to dry; bang in the peg to the point covered by the white paint, banging the next peg in 10 ft away, making certain its top is level with the other. You can soon find out when this is so by the use of the board and spirit level. It is the white mark on the peg which will show you how much extra soil you need to get the ground level. So by moving some soil from place to place and by keeping on with the pegging and spirit level, the job will gradually get done perfectly.

Just one word of warning. There is a great danger of taking all the surface soil away from the highest part of the plot in order to level out the lowest part, and the result is that the high parts will do badly because seed will have to be sown on the subsoil. The low parts on the other hand will do well because there will be a double layer of soil there. So if such drastic treatment as removing 6 or 7in of soil from one of the lawns to the other is needed, the plan must be to dig away the surface soil there, then remove 6in of subsoil below—and put the surface soil back. Next the gardener must go down to the lower part, dig out the surface soil there, put in the subsoil from the top area, and then put the soil back again. This means, as will be seen, a tremendous amount of work, and usually puts anyone off the idea of bothering about a truly level lawn. Always use a rake and roller to help with the levelling.

There is never any need to dig deeply. Forking the ground over to a depth of 3in will do admirably. During this process, if the soil is very heavy add sand, coke ashes (not coal), or in fact any gritty material of this kind that will help it open up. If, on the other hand, the land is very sandy, peat humus or peat moss will be used instead, forked in at four bucketsful to the square yard. It is quite a good thing to add a little old soot to a light sandy soil as this helps to darken it and so make it warmer.

While forking, be sure to remove all the perennial weeds. It is worth while spending hours and hours getting out every bit of couch or convolvulus or bindweed or creeping thistle or whatever it may be. Don't just say well, a little bit won't matter. A little bit will matter! The alternative is to treat the weeds in the spring as advised in Chapters 3 and 4. Don't lime the ground at this time; lime only encourages the clovers, and a good lawn consists of fine grasses, not clovers.

After forking, tread the ground or give it a light rolling. Then do the raking carefully so as to leave the surface very fine and level. Every particle of soil must be finer than a grain of wheat. It is usually necessary to rake, then roll, and rake again. Sometimes it is a good plan to give two or three rollings and two or three rakings, and yet never to rake or roll when the weather is wet. No one can satisfactorily work on sticky ground.

Leave the soil alone and allow the annual weeds to grow: there should be a very good harvest—hundreds of them will rapidly appear and it will not be long before the carefully raked piece of ground is as green as grass. On a nice warm day go over it and hoe all the weeds down, leaving them on the surface to die. There is no need to rake them off—the sun will kill them where they lie. Leave the lawn again, if you can, for another week or fortnight, and so get a second crop of weeds. These can be hoed off in their turn, and thus it is possible to start the lawn with the majority of the weed seeds having germinated so that there isn't much competition with the grass seeds that are going to be sown.

The alternative, as has been already said with regard to perennial weeds, is to water all the plants with a poison which kills them all by eliminating the chlorophyll (ie, the green colouring matter) in the leaves.

SOWING THE SEED

Don't buy grass seed haphazardly from a local shop—buy lawn seed by name, just as vegetables seeds are bought by name. If you buy a few pence worth of 'lawn seed', you will have no idea what it contains. The best lawn-seed mixture consists of five parts Chewings fescue, two parts creeping red fescue and three parts New Zealand bent. Another prescription, which omits the bents, consists of one part fine-leaved sheep's fescue, two parts Chewings fescue and one part sea-washed fescue. The first mixture, however, makes the quicker lawn and smothers out the weeds more effectively. Never use too much seed; 5lb of seed per 100sq yd is sufficient when you are using 'the bents', and 7lb of seed per 100sq yd when using the other mixture.

Sow the seed evenly all over the surface of the ground; to do this quite a good tip is to mix the seed with sand first of all, and after sowing rake the whole area over carefully. If it is dry run the roller over the ground afterwards to compress it. Birds can be a great nuisance in towns —they seem to flock down in great numbers to eat the seeds. There are, however, substances that repel birds which can be mixed with the seeds before sowing.

LATER CARE

Once the lawn has been sown, be patient. Don't cut the young grass until it is at least 4in high, and then it is better to do the first cut with a scythe. The first cutting with the lawn mower will be done about a fortnight after that, or maybe three weeks. This time see that the bottom-plate is fairly high. Never cut low for the first four cuts. After this set the blades lower, and so produce the perfect lawn.

Rolling

A lawn never needs a roller heavier than 200lb at any time of the year. The aim of rolling should be to keep the surface level: it should never aim at squashing bumps and filling up depressions. It is best done in the late spring or early summer, as it is apt to consolidate the soil too much when it is very wet.

Spiking and raking

A lawn when mown regularly tends to form a dense mat and consolidation of the soil is bound to take place. It is necessary therefore from time to time to aerate the ground by means of spikes. This spiking is best done with a long-tined fork which should be plunged into the soil perpendicularly to its full depth. If the fork is used in this way, 18in apart, the aeration will be sufficient. Spiking should be done in the spring. It will ensure a greater resistance during drought and is a definite check against the growth of moss.

Every autumn after removing the fallen leaves the lawn ought to be raked over with a stiff-tined wire rake. This raking removes the creeping weeds, dead moss and grass. This can be done mechanically if you can rent a machine. Scratch up the top $\frac{1}{8}$in or so and thus improve the surface. It is a good idea to sprinkle the surface afterwards with fine compost at the rate of say 3–4lb per square yard.

Worms

Worms, though very valuable in all other parts of the garden, can be a nuisance on the lawn, for as they carry out their normal functions they bring worm casts to the surface. These make it difficult to mow properly and are a great nuisance when lawns are going to be used for clock golf, croquet or bowls. There is no difficulty in eliminating the worms by the use of a metaldehyde meal, which should be applied all over the surface of the lawn at 4oz per square yard in the spring and again if necessary in the early summer. After the meal has been applied a good flooding should be given with water, and the worms will come to the surface in great numbers. They should be raked up and put on the compost heap.

Patching

Where a bare patch occurs in a lawn there is little difficulty in renovating it. Rake it over, and apply a grass-seed mixture at the rate of 1oz of seed to a 5in pot full of sterilised soil. This should be sprinkled evenly over the raked area to a depth of ¼in or so, and lightly rolled. If the seeds are germinated a few days ahead by being damped, the result is firstly that the birds do not care for it as much, and secondly that the patch is furnished with fresh grass more quickly. To achieve prior germination, add 2lb of good grass seed to 1 bushel of fine soil, and spread it out on a concrete floor—preferably in a shed. Give it a light watering, and the seeds are stimulated and encouraged to germinate.

Camellia japonica, var magnoliae flora (*Harry Smith*)

Watering

In drought periods in summer, it may be necessary to water the lawn. This should always be done early in the evening when the heat of the day has passed. Use a hose, fitted with a sprinkler, and see that the water is thrown well up into the air so that it is aerated and thus moistens the land properly and gradually. Never water a lawn unless absolutely necessary. Once watering is started it must be continued once a week during a dry spell.

If, however, the lawn is new it may be necessary, in dry weather, to water almost every day till it has become firmly established. Lawns that are newly turfed have to be kept watered also, till the grass is well rooted into the ground below. Watering is also necessary for lawns that are given hard wear by tennis players. Remember though each locality has specific watering problems and laws which govern the use of water.

Mowing

On an established lawn, the grass should never be allowed to grow longer than 2in or it starts to deteriorate. Keep cutting regularly, therefore, to prevent the grass getting to this height. Normally this will mean cutting twice a week during the growing season if it is to keep in perfect condition—or once a week at the minimum. Always sweep the lawn clear of stones and worm casts or else the cutting blades of the machine will be injured.

Mow occasionally on fine days during the winter months, for grass continues to grow except in really freezing weather. If a certain amount of cutting isn't done, say once a month, it becomes untidy and ragged-looking. See that the mowing machine is in perfect condition. Brush it clean and oil it well before putting it away, and have the blades sharpened each winter and the bottom plate also.

Feeding

The compost gardener will realise that as he cuts the lawn week by week and removes the lawn mowings, he is robbing the lawn of organic matter. He will therefore dress the lawn with fine organic matter in the spring each year applying either the brown powdery compost he has made himself or natural compost, peat humus. The lawn needs a heavy dressing, ie 3 or 4 bucketsful to the square yard, and in addition fish manure or meat and bone meal at 3oz to the square yard is useful. This must be applied evenly all over the lawn to ensure that there is no scorching.

Keen composters often refuse to use a mower which collects the clippings. They use instead a rotary cutter, as mentioned in Chapter 3 and allow the mowings to lie on the lawn and be pulled in by the worms. The worms in this case are not eliminated, being allowed to do the work of (a) aerating the soil and (b) adding plant foods naturally. This means that any unsightly worm casts will quickly be distributed by the cutter of the machine. If you find that a rotary cutter leaves your lawn too untidy, and prefer to use a cutter that collects the clippings, then compost all these properly and put them back on the lawn as a brown powder each April, as I do!

A CHAMOMILE LAWN

By the sea, or even in the country, a chamomile lawn instead of a grass lawn can be extremely attractive. It will never go yellow in the driest of summers and in fact keeps beautifully dark green month after month throughout the year. It will be pleasantly soft and fragrant—old country people claim that it is health-giving.

The important thing is not to grow just any kind of chamomile, but to plant what is known as the Treneague strain. Most of the old-fashioned chamomile lawns are grown from *Anthemis nobilis,* which is continually flowering and is apt to grow long and lanky, needing regular cutting. But the Treneague strain never flowers and *never* requires to be cut. It spreads quietly all over the soil; the plants don't, as it were, raise their heads! Further, the creeping growths root themselves into the soil, forming a thick sward or carpet so that weeds are easily controlled. It is said that this strain comes from a 'sport' from the gardens of Buckingham Palace in London, where there is a huge chamomile lawn. It is not a good thing to mix it with other chamomile plants—it should be grown on its own. It is not particular as to soil or locality.

Buy the plants and put them in firmly, 5in apart, in clean land. This can be done at almost any time of year. Keep the land free from weeds until the smothering sward develops. Give a top dressing of compost each autumn, using about 2 bucketsful to the square yard.

A small town garden. (*Harry Smith*)

Red currants. (*Harry Smith*)

A border and well furnished greenhouse at Arkley Manor.
(*Author*)

Luxuriant flowering shrubs at Killerton Gardens.
(*E. H. Lumb*)

10

THE SEASIDE GARDEN

IT seems fairly obvious that the main problem that affects a garden by the sea is the sea itself. The salt spray at certain times of the year can be very serious indeed; the leaves, the plants, the branches of the trees and shrubs and even the soil may have fairish quantities of sodium chloride deposited on them. One has therefore to grow trees and plants which don't mind salt or will at least put up with it. One must always be thinking of the roots below ground as well as the aerial parts of the plants.

Salt then could be enemy number one—or it might be a friend in disguise.

The second big problem is undoubtedly winds. Gales can be quite serious in areas well away from the sea, but in seaside gardens there may be storms and heavy salt-laden gales of the 80 to 100 miles per hour type, which can do great damage. This is not only the immediately obvious tearing-out of leaves in the summer, or blowing over of the border shrubs in winter, but also scorching of vegetables and fruits.

Thirdly, the coastal gardener often has to cope with a sandy soil, and he must therefore be prepared to mulch heavily and to adopt some simple system of overhead irrigation.

Of course, seaside gardens, like others, differ from one locality to another. There's all the difference, for instance, between the lovely garden I once saw at Aghada in Southern Ireland and a beautiful garden at Logan in the West of Scotland. It is obvious that where the Gulf Stream touches the west coast of Scotland there is a definite warmth which makes the gardens in that area able to grow trees and shrubs that couldn't possibly be grown even as nearby as the east coast of Scotland for instance. On the coasts of Cornwall there are areas which are very sheltered indeed and where sub-tropical plants can grow; other parts of Cornwall can be tremendously windy month after month.

The climate on the North American coast varies even more dramatically than in the British Isles, from the tropics of Florida to arctic Alaska. The sea has a moderating effect upon the adjacent coastal lands. England, situated as far north as Labrador, has quite a mild, stable climate while Montana varies widely from winter to summer. Great bodies of water exert a stabilising effect by stretching out a cool spring and moderating the autumn thus preventing early frosts.

It's impossible to lay down hard and fast rules, but it is possible to say that because a garden is near the sea it is less likely to be damaged by frost, early or late, than a similar garden inland. The Great Lakes, not salty but none the less inland seas, alter the climate sufficiently to permit large-scale grape-growing on the adjacent land. Many countries have districts well known for being 'early land'; the local gardeners can get earlier results; they will know for instance that their dahlias will go on flowering much longer in the autumn, because Jack Frost's icy fingers will probably not be appearing until well on in October. Nor is it every plant that minds the salt, and so later on details are given of those that are very happy by the

Vegetable marrow (*Bernard Alfieri*)

sea, such as wallflowers, which seem to love the salt spray, and tulips which seem happier under salty conditions than other types of bulbs. In areas where the highest rainfall can be expected, a good soaking will often wash away much of the salty deposits. On other coasts, where rainfall is light, the shrubs and trees can suffer all the worse.

One can always learn much from other people's mistakes, as well as from local gardeners. When settling down in a seaside area, take a walk around and see what plants are succeeding and what seem to fail. Your nearest nurseryman will know a tremendous amount about what will grow and what will not. It would be a good thing to cultivate his friendship and get his advice—he is undoubtedly a very busy man, but being a good gardener he will be a kindly fellow.

Start your new garden by thinking about shelter, by deciding what fence is going to be provided and what trees and hedges are going to be put in. It isn't always necessary to plant a windbreak too thickly: give the specimens room to develop, remembering that their function will be to 'filter' the gales and prevent them from 'charging at' your plants with tremendous fury. Successful market gardeners often put wire-netting barriers across an open field because they find that this breaks up the main wind into little eddies.

THE IMPORTANCE OF HUMUS

In Chapter 2 the whole question of compost and composting is dealt with fully, but it is important to highlight the value of humus in seaside soil, for most seaside gardens, like town gardens, are particularly lacking in this 'bridge between life and death'. Again, the older gardens are usually the worst. Years ago, because it was difficult to get farmyard manure, people tended to rely on chemical fertilisers; the result was that the humus tended to 'burn out'. Nobody seemed to know how to make up for the lack of dung which the old gardeners used to use until the advent of composting and peat humus, though by the sea you would have thought that they would have realised that seaweed was ideal. Most seaside gardens have powdery eroded soil which needs to be fed with organic matter, and as elsewhere, if the garden owner cannot make sufficient compost even with the use of seaweed, then he must buy peat humus and use it in addition or instead.

Those who live by the sea can usually get hold of plenty of seaweed; and it is the one organic manure that contains more potash than phosphates and is in addition rich in most of the trace elements required by plants. Actually in many seaside resorts seaweed is regarded as a menace and a nuisance because the large deposits on the beaches make it unpleasant, people say, for the visitors. There ought never to be any seaweed left on beaches, for all the garden-owners nearby should be dashing down to collect this valuable manure to put on their compost heaps.

Seaweed can either be rotted down on its own, 6in layer by 6in layer, as with ordinary compost, or it can be used on the normal compost heap if preferred, mixed with the lawn mowings, the leaves, coffee grounds, banana peel and whatever has been collected from home or garden. It fortunately decomposes quickly, and when used in the soil becomes a quick-acting manure. It is also, of course, free from weed seeds. The writer when he uses composted seaweed alone usually adds bone meal at the rate of 4–5oz to the square yard, because analysis shows that seaweed manure may be deficient in phosphates.

11

THE COMPOST TECHNIQUE FOR WINDOW BOXES

IT is possible today to buy window boxes already made up, but very often they do not, for some reason or another, fit the window or windowsill perfectly. Most people, therefore, prefer to make their own, to fit their space and to suit the style of the house or apartment. It is nice to be able to use cedar, teak or redwood and then not have to paint the wood and yet know it will last almost for ever. Whether the box is wood, metal or concrete, you can use a metal container inside it, having another as a spare: one will be actually growing flowers on the windowsill while the other is being planted up or prepared somewhere indoors, even at the local nurseryman's. When the first show of flowers in window box 1 is over, it is a simple matter to lift it out, by means of the two folding handles at either end of the box, and to slip the newly-planted box 2 in its place. These metal boxes, therefore, can be regarded as linings to the more permanent box.

Don't forget that the first thing, once you have your box, is to make certain that it is firmly fixed. There is nothing more likely to bring you trouble than your window box landing on the head of a passer-by! A householder has his responsibilities in that direction.

The business of watering has also to be borne in mind. Some arrangements ought to be made for the excess water to drain away into a shallow tray inserted under the drainage holes. One can easily see that no one is underneath when the watering is being done, but the trouble is that it usually takes some time before the water seeps through the soil and it may splash over the windowsill just when some fair lady is passing.

MAKING A WINDOW BOX

Wood is still the most usual material for window boxes, and it is a very easy medium to work with; hard-wood boxes will, of course, outlast those made with the softer woods.

The planks to be used should be $\frac{5}{8}$in to $1\frac{1}{8}$in thick, and the length should be such that the box fits closely to the frames of the windows so that these help to keep it in position. The good workman will take the trouble to dovetail the ends of the box together, but where this is impossible screws should be used to do the fixing because nails are unreliable.

The inside of the box should be at least 7in deep (and preferably 10in) and at least 6in wide. Holes should be bored in the bottom of the box 8in apart, in zigzag fashion, to allow for drainage. Sloped wedges should be used to keep the bottom of the window box just above the shallow metal tray, allowing excess water to get away quickly; I have seen rubber door-stops used for this purpose with success. Some people prefer to have the wedge so arranged that the box has a slight tilt towards one corner where they bore what may be described as a main drainage hole, which drips into a suspended can. This can is removed directly the drip has ceased, three hours or so after watering.

Char the inside of the box with a red-hot iron or blow-torch. If this is impossible it may be soaked in a proprietary substance like Cuprinol preservative liquid. Never treat the inside of the box with creosote or tar as this causes trouble for years to come: the roots of plants cannot bear to come into contact with either of these substances and the fumes they give off will inhibit the production of root hairs. Unless it is redwood, teak or cedar, the outside of it

Gentiana sino ornata (*Harry Smith*)

should be painted; a coat of red lead may be used followed by two coats of a paint of the colour desired. The general colouring of the window box may fit in with the general painting scheme of the house or, of course, may be a contrast.

It is possible to fit a window box to a window that has no sill, special brackets having to be inserted into the outside wall to take the weight. One firm that used to do a considerable amount of this kind of work used to make a box 3ft long, 9in wide and 8½in deep. This opened at the back and was supplied complete with what they called an earth box, 2ft 10½in by 8in by 7in. This earth box could be of metal or an aluminium alloy, and it would fit exactly inside the wooden box. If preferred the main box could be of aluminium and the inside earth box would be of wood.

Do be sure that your window box is properly made before attempting to put in any compost or soil. If it is glued, see that you cannot pull it apart; if it is screwed, see that the screw heads have not broken off; and if it is nailed, make sure that the nails cannot pull out with the strain. It is always better to fit a box while it is still empty, because once it is filled with soil it is far more difficult to handle: this may sound obvious, but there have been those who have tried to do the work with the boxes fully loaded!

FILLING AND PLANTING

See that plenty of broken crocks are placed over the holes in the box, making certain to put the concave pieces with the hollow downwards over the drainage holes, so as to prevent the soil from washing through while allowing the water to escape. Town gardeners often find it difficult to get such crocks, even though there may be plenty to spare in a country garden; oyster shells, which many good fish stores can supply, may be used instead, or even stones. Over the top should be placed a generous layer of peat humus. This again helps with the drainage, acting as a sponge, holding the moisture and yet being willing to release it as it is required by the plant roots. Any horticultural speciality shop in the town will supply peat in this sort of quantity, and the layer may be put, 2in thick, right over the bottom of the box (I mean 2in when damped and fully firmed).

Now we come to the actual soil in which the plants are to grow. There are firms who will supply the right type of soil mixture—such as Alex All-Purpose Compost or Peat-Lite. The advantages are that they are standard products which, when unmixed, will store indefinitely; they are easy to prepare and almost ready to use; they are excellent rooting mediums (that is, after all, the prime function of such a medium); the absence of stones and rough material makes for easier and quicker transplanting; they not only sustain growth but sometimes even promote faster growth; they give more 'root room' because less space is taken up with bulky insert materials like stones, etc, which would otherwise be needed to keep the soil drainage open, and therefore larger plants can be grown; owing to the high peat content, moisture-retention is very high; and that compared to a loam compost, they afford less danger of root-scorch on drying out or accidental over-strong feeding.

It is important to moisten the mixture before it is put into the window boxes or tubs. Some gardeners think it is sufficient to wet it in the container before sowing or planting, but this is wrong. Moisten it lightly—mix some dry with some wet medium—and leave it in a slightly compacted heap for several hours to allow moisture to spread evenly through. Conditioning will enable it to 'take' water subsequently and also impart extra 'structure' to it.

You can, of course, make your own potting material which is every bit as good as the commercial mix and more natural. A standard mix would be as follows: four parts compost or peat humus to one part sharp builder's sand or, for those who have not yet made compost and cannot find peat humus, use equal parts of general-purpose sterilised soil, sharp sand and peat moss. You can vary the mix according to the needs of a plant by increasing the amount of sand for desert plants, and increasing the amount of peat moss for plants that like a moist soil.

When filling the window boxes be very careful with the corners, because it is there that the soil is apt to be loose: thus when water is added it rushes to these corners; the central parts of the compost in the box is not damp. Aim to put in the soil layer by layer until the box is filled to within about an inch of the top. It is then a good plan to leave the compost to settle for a week or so before planting.

Do not overfirm. When seed-sowing, firm lightly with a presser board, mainly to obtain a level surface. When inserting plants, fill and plant with minimum firming. Water in afterwards, using sufficient water just to drain, perhaps giving more next day or so if the weather is very bright; but avoid over-watering during the early stages of plant establishment, because the soil is loose at this time.

A top dressing or mulching of compost or peat humus should be added after the plants are in position, or, when seeds are sown, after the seedlings are well through the ground.

WATERING

Naturally, some types of window boxes dry out more quickly than others, and those on the sunny side of a house need more water than those in the shade. The humidity of the local atmosphere also makes a great deal of difference. The difficulty about a window box is that all sides are exposed to drying influences, and in consequence evaporation is much faster than in a flower bed. By and large, it can be said that watering should be carried out every twenty-four hours, preferably in the evening or early in the morning. Don't think that because it has rained hard the boxes will not need watering: too often the boxes never get rained on at all, being protected by the eaves of the house or the way of the wind.

Don't splash when watering—use a small spout to a can that can be directed around the roots of the plants. There is no need to flood the box, just water so that the soil or compost becomes moist and keep an eye, if you can, on water that may be running out from the drainage holes. More water has to be given, naturally, after hot days than after damp days and when there is plenty of wind the soil dries out even quicker. Once you get to know your window box well you will have a very good idea of how much water to apply on each occasion.

Never allow the soil in the box to become dried out, for once it has set, so to speak, in a solid block it is very difficult to moisten again. The compost or soil seems to leave the edges of the box and a kind of caked brick gets formed in the centre with a ¼in air space all round. Such a 'brick' is almost impossible to break down. It is honestly a question of watering regularly, and when you are away on holiday someone must be deputed to do it for you. Also, syringe the plants over, not only to clean them—important in sooty areas—but as an aid to controlling red spider and other pests.

CULTIVATION AND FEEDING

Once the plants are in position and growing well there is little to do other than to pick off the dead flowers and yellowing leaves regularly. Once a week or so the surface of the box should be lightly stirred with a small hand fork, though this is never so necessary when the mulching of compost is in position. If and when some of the mulch disappears it is sensible to apply another dressing. A very useful little tool for stirring the surface from time to time is an old carving fork.

If plants get tall and tend to topple over, the best method of support is to push some twiggy sticks into the soil.

Some like to use an organic fertiliser like a fish manure and to apply this all over the surface of the box at the rate of ½oz per square foot, about once a month. It is, however, better on the whole to use a liquid manure; the town gardener can easily buy bottles of this. You can make your own liquid fertiliser by steeping dried dung in water and giving weekly doses of the manure tea.

Some people use a compost mixture in their window boxes for three or four years without bothering to renew it. They claim that by feeding the soil regularly and applying the mulch, they have retained its humus content and its 'vitality'. The alternative, of course, to taking the whole of the soil out of the box is just to remove part of it, say the top inch or so. This might conveniently be removed, and an inch or two of the fresh mixture be put back in its place.

Helleborous foetidus (*Harry Smith*)

THE PLANTS

Use fair-sized plants, well hardened-off; always go for the short sturdy ones with a nice deep colour to the foliage. Buy them if possible with a good ball of soil to the roots, and with a little trowel make the necessary hole in the compost, planting the ball without disturbing it, then pressing the soil firmly round about. Many people like to use drooping plants towards the front of the window box so that they hang over the front panel and produce quite a beautiful effect. I have used the Golden Gleam nasturtium in this way and find it ideal for the purpose.

Ivy-leaved geraniums are also useful for the draping scheme and they have the advantage of blooming almost continuously. Most people tend to overplant a box, rather than underplant, and there is every excuse for this, but crowding can be a cause of trouble later on, because the plants have no room to spread and grow. So don't have geraniums closer than say 18in apart and give the lobelia which you may be using for the front of the box 6in of room. There are some plants, of course, which don't spread, typical examples being the bulbs like hyacinths or daffodils.

The lists that follow include plants for the autumn and spring window-box planting, the aim being to have a succession. I have also suggested plants that prefer shady positions and those that like the sunny spots. Choosing the plants you like, work out a plan to suit the background or the position or even the year. Traditionally, most window boxes have been planted with red, white and blue, but nowadays people range more widely: try gold, scarlet and purple, or lavender, gold and blue, or blue, white and yellow, or red and yellow alone: or, of course, just a regular mixture. It is your house and your window box and have it as you like: but do look at it from outside as well as from inside, and remember that it has to face the criticisms of those who come and see you as well as the remarks of those who pass by. A window box has to be double-fronted, so to speak!

Never forget scent when planning a window box. There are a number of suitable plants which, as the following lists show, are beautifully fragrant. Some, like nicotiana (the tobacco plant), are gloriously scented in the evening hours and can be planted in the shady boxes with great effect. Quite a good idea is just to have one plant at either end of the box. For early morning scent, there is little to beat the common white alyssum, which can be used as an edging plant or even just at the two ends.

The night-scented stock does not look at all pretty in the day time for its flowers close, but is attractively fragrant on a summer evening when you have the window open and cool breezes are coming in, and this is one of the few cases where I would not mind sowing just a little seed in any three places in the box, just for the delightful evening perfume. I mention other scented plants, like wallflowers and hyacinths, in the lists below.

The following list applies to a temperate climate without severe frosts in the winter. In areas with harsher weather you will have to wait until spring to plant your window box with seedlings you have started indoors or with plants from the local greenhouse.

AUTUMN PLANTING

Variety	*Flowering period*	*Cultivation hints*
1. Sunny position		
Aubretia	April–June	plant October
Chionodoxa	March	plant September
Crocus	February–April	plant September

Variety	*Flowering period*	*Cultivation hints*
2. Sunny position—scented		
Hyacinth	spring	plant September–October
Siberian Wallflower	spring and early summer	plant March
Tulip	March–April	plant October
3. Shady position		
Aucuba	evergreen	plant October–November
Creeping Jenny	June–September	plant spring
Crocus	spring	plant September
Ivy	evergreen	plant October
Olearia	July–September, June	plant September–November or April
Dahlia	late summer and autumn	plant mid-May
Geranium	summer	plant out early June
Marguerite	summer	plant out early June
Petunia	July–August	plant out early June
Salvia	late summer and autumn	plant out early June
Stock	summer	plant out late May or early June
Verbena	summer	plant out May
Zinnia	summer	plant out May

SPRING SOWING OR PLANTING

1. Sunny position		
Annual Chrysanthemum	summer	plant out May
Antirrhinum (Snapdragon)	July	plant April–May
Campanula	July	plant March–April
Wallflower	spring	plant out firmly September–October
2. Sunny position—scented		
Nasturtium	summer	sow seeds 1in deep in April
Geranium	summer	plant out May
Sweet Alyssum	summer	sow seeds April
3. Shady position		
Begonia	summer	plant out early June
Calceolaria	June–July	plant March
Creeping Jenny	June–September	plant March
Ferns, such as Alpine polypody	all the year	plant April
Fuchsia	July	plant April
Lobelia	summer	plant March–April

Variety	*Flowering period*	*Cultivation hints*
4. Shady position—scented		
Tobacco Plant	summer	plant out early June
Viola	summer	plant March or April
5. Sunny position—trailers		
Campanula	July	plant April. Good in hanging baskets
Canary Creeper	summer	plant out May
Cobaea	summer	plant out in early June
Hop	hardy flowers	plant out May or June
Ivy-leaved Geranium	summer	plant out early June
Lobelia trailing varieties	September	plant out June
Morning Glory	summer	plant out June
Nasturtium	summer	sow seeds 1in deep, in April
6. Shady position—trailers		
Creeping Jenny	hardy flowers	plant October–March
Nepeta	summer	plant October or March
Periwinkle	May–September	plant October or April
Saxifrage	summer	plant October–March
Tradescantia	May–September	plant October–November or March–April
Variegated Ivy	evergreen	plant October–March
7. Climbers for permanent planting		
Ivy	does not flower	October to March
Virginia Creeper	does not flower	plant winter
Vitis	does not flower	plant autumn

12

THE ORGANIC GARDENER'S GUIDE TO PEST AND DISEASE CONTROL

THERE is no doubt that trees, shrubs and plants grown on organic methods (which must include non-inversion of the soil) are far less liable to attacks of pests and diseases than similar plants grown on constantly dug and forked soil, fed with chemical fertilisers. Truly healthy plants are like truly healthy people—they have a natural inborn resistance.

On the other hand it cannot be said truthfully that compost-grown plants are immune from the troubles that beset 'the flora' as a whole. Organic gardeners must adopt preventive measures which are not harmful to friendly predators and which will do no harm to human beings. The real aim is not to upset the balance of nature or indeed produce automatically resistant strains of certain pests which could be more virulent in their attacks than were the original insects. Sprays like DDT have indeed produced just this reaction. If the gardener is not alert to this aid he may receive from natural predators, he may spray too early and unnecessarily. When a keen gardener found, as he told me, five or six aphides on a rose bush in my garden one day in July, I said I was glad because my dear little friends the ladybirds must have something to eat! We are, in my opinion, far too quick to exterminate what we term a pest—without pausing to see whether the normal predators are available near by to do the work nature intends them to do.

PREDATORS

We must learn first of all to recognise the normal predators found in the garden. There are three main predators: (1) the ladybird, (2) the hover fly and (3) the lace-wing fly. Nearly everyone knows the ladybird but few recognise the nigger which is the larvae or youngster of the ladybird. This is black in colour with maybe a few orange or red dots on it. I always say it looks like a tiny alligator.

The hover fly looks like a little wasp, which instead of busily flying about from place to place just hovers in the pathway in the sun, or over the lawn, making no noise and yet with its wings fluttering like the propellers of an aeroplane.

Not all gardens are blessed with plenty of hover flies, and it is a good thing to know how to encourage them because they are hearty consumers of aphides. One way to do this is to sow a row or two of buckwheat, say, as an edging to the vegetable garden, or put in a dozen or so seeds to form one or two clumps in the flower border. The buckwheat plants are quite decorative and for some reason or another the hover flies love them and seem to feed on them; whether they really do this or not, it is worthwhile troubling to make them welcome.

The lace-wing fly is much more difficult to describe, but most people have noticed this dainty insect, which will sometimes be attracted indoors by the lights at night. It has a light

Bitter pit and stony pit in apples and pears

The apples may be covered or partly covered with brown marks or depressions, and when the skin is removed brown marks are found to penetrate the flesh. This does not spoil the flavour of the whole fruit, though the individual 'pits' are bitter to the taste.

In the case of pears, the sunken areas are dark green and hard. The fruits are usually misshapen and the tissue at the sunken spots is stony and hard. The precise causes of these maladies have not been discovered, but severe pruning undoubtedly predisposes the trees, as does heavy feeding with nitrogenous fertilisers. Fluctuations of the supply of water is a contributory factor, especially in the case of trees grown against walls.

The answer in the latter case is to mulch with sedge peat and apply overhead irrigation in the summer. It always helps to give wood ashes at ½lb to the square yard in February each year—this ensures sufficient potash in the soil. Varieties that are susceptible to these troubles include Bramley Seedling, James Grieve, Cox's Orange Pippin, Blenheim Orange and Allington Pippin, in the case of apples; and Beurré Hardy, Doyenné du Comice, Pitmaston Duchess and Winter Nelis, in the case of pears.

Black fly

On broad beans, runner beans, French beans, etc. These live on the spindle bushes (*Euonymus europaeus*) in the winter and they may be tackled there by spraying with nicotine in February, for they migrate to the beans in March and April. When first seen on the beans, spray thoroughly with liquid derris.

Black spot on roses

Covering the ground with compost 1in deep does prevent the spores of the black-spot disease from blowing up from the soil to the leaves. Mixing up an 'elder tea' with elderberry leaves in boiling water is sometimes claimed to prevent the disease and control mildew as well. (We haven't used this at Arkley Manor as our compost mulchings do the trick.)

Canker

This is a disease occurring principally on apples. The fungus eats away the bark and produces a rough-edged wound. Cut out the diseased areas carefully with a sharp knife, paring it all away. Then paint the wound with tree paint. Always control the woolly aphis, the pest which produces cotton-wool-like tufts on the branches, as this carries the spores of canker with it and can cause infection.

Carrot fly/onion fly

Both species of fly lay their eggs along the rows, attracted by the scent of carrot or onion, and the maggots then attack the crops. Growing the two crops in alternate rows mystifies the two pests as a rule! Growing parsley on either side of onions will also usually be effective; the alternative is to plant onion sets, instead of sowing seed—the onion fly seldom attacks these. Sprinkling naphthalene in between the rows of carrots will create a smell enough to keep the carrot flies away: a very slight hoeing after this will increase the smell. Another method is to cover the earth around the plant with a thin layer of wood ashes after the seedlings are about 3in tall.

Caterpillars

Always tackle these when young, whatever the species, and whether on gooseberry bushes, cabbages, or apples and plums. Spray with derris or pyrethrum.

Clematis stem wilt

Grow as many stems as possible coming up from soil level. The idea is to layer some shoots and they will root quite quickly, especially if plenty of fine sedge peat and silver sand is worked into the soil first. When the stem is just buried in the compost, scrape away the bark a little and cut carefully into the stem upwards so as to split it, but not to cut if off. Dust the split part thoroughly with a hormone rooting-dust, and peg down with a bent wire shaped like a hairpin. Cover with the peaty soil and sand and keep this just damp. In this way you will have a clematis with many stems which will never fail you—for if one stem does get 'wilt', the others will carry on.

Club-root disease/Cabbage-root maggot

Two quite different troubles but they often appear together. The Good Gardeners' Association has been carrying out trials and the results so far show that there is no perfect remedy. The Association has tried out all the recommended cures, ie rhubarb, acetic acid, elderberry leaves and so on! The best answer at the moment is the use of a mixture of egg shells and wood ashes mixed on a 50/50 basis and a teaspoonful put into the holes at planting time. Some people have successfully combated the problems with wood ash placed around the stem of the plant after transplanting or, if directly seeded, after the seedlings put out their second leaves.

Green fly

On fruit trees and bushes, or on bush or rambler roses. Spray with pyrethrum or derris, having made certain first that the predators are not on the job. In many cases the aphides collect under the leaves and cause them to pucker or curl.

Leaf miner in chrysanthemums

Make up a good brew of soot and water, by putting a large handful of coal soot in a bucket of boiling water and stirring well. Allow to cool and then water the chrysanthemums with it once a week. It gives the leaves a bitter taste which the fly doesn't like when she comes to lay her eggs. You can also spray with a nicotine wash on a warm sunny day—also once a week. Nicotine is very poisonous and must be kept away from children. Nicotine aerosols can be obtained from garden centres as a rule, and this can be used in the greenhouse as well as outside.

Leaf mould in tomatoes

A very common disease of tomatoes, particularly under glass. It usually occurs in July and August. The pale-grey fungus appears as a mould, first of all on the underside of the leaves in large spots. This fungus changes to tawny-olive and finally to purple. The upper surfaces of the leaves turn pale yellow and then reddish-browh. The leaves next become brown and brittle and finally die. The fungus spreads most rapidly under humid conditions.

Grow the immune varieties which are offered by most seedsmen.

Leaf spot or blight

On celery. Discoloured areas are found on the leaves in which little black 'bodies' are seen. The spots increase until the whole leaf is affected. It then withers away, turns grey in color and rots. This trouble usually starts in July. Buy from a seedsman who sells 'treated' seed, or soak the seed yourself in a weak solution of formaldehyde for 24 hours (1 part formaline to 300 parts water). In the garden, if the disease does break out, spray with Bordeaux mixture. Cover the leaves well with the wash and repeat the dose again twice at intervals of 14 days.

Dwarf green curled kale (*Harry Smith*)

Maggots

In raspberries, loganberries, blackberries, etc. The maggots are the larvae of little brown beetles which lay eggs in the opened flowers. Kill these beetles by spraying with the non-poisonous rotenone or derris: do this when the flowers are opening.

Mildew

On cabbages, cauliflower, sprouts and the like. This mildew attacks the young plants and seedlings. The leaves turn yellowish-green and, when examined, white downy patches are seen on the under surfaces. To prevent and control this disease, spray with liver of sulphur. Dissolve 1oz of potassium sulphide in 2½ gallons of water.

Mint rust

This disease occurs wherever mint is grown. The plants attacked can be noticed in the spring and summer because the shoots are distorted and abnormally thick. Before long yellowish-orange cushions appear on the stems and leaves. These produce innumerable spores which are distributed to other plants which they infect. Rust spreads like an epidemic in the summer. In the winter, dark brown or almost black spores are formed.

Burn off the mint tops in late September or early October. Use dry straw for this purpose and produce a rapid fire so as to burn the stems and the leaves. It is well worthwhile washing the roots that are to be replanted outdoors in plenty of clean water. An even more effective method is to subject the roots to hot-water treatment. They should be immersed in a bath of hot water maintained at a temperature of 112° F for ten minutes.

Moles

Many of us know the exasperation that comes from discovering one morning that a nice neat lawn—or a newly-planted row of raspberry runners—has been ruinously disrupted overnight by a mere mole. The mole is a tunneller, and as he tunnels the worms and the insects in the vicinity of his work feel the vibrations acutely and they flee, many of them coming out of the ground in their agitation. He is a wonderful soil engineer, and can easily dig a 22-yard tunnel of his own size in 24 hours, even under a lawn where there may be roots to impede his way. He burrows, of course, because he is looking for food; in fact, he eats half his own weight of worms and insects each day. Apparently he can feel vibrations which are set up by all insects, and particularly worms, though how far away he can sense them is the subject of study at the moment. There are evidently thousands of nerve fibres in the nose of a mole and these are extremely sensitive. A cat has six nerve fibres going to each whisker, but a mole has forty. He can tell in a split second the slightest change in air pressure—so when the mole is rushing down a tunnel in the dark he 'feels' and knows exactly where the bends are and so never bashes his little pink nose.

He lives alone, very independent, for most of his four-year span, and will fight to the death any other mole he meets. He does, however, have the mating urge in the early spring, and babies are born in April, May and June, in nests dug out under the soil. When the young do their first tunnelling they are a bit zigzaggy and often too near the surface so that they are eaten by owls, foxes, badgers and even crows. Moles will take care to make 'air filters' every 3 or 4ft in their tunnels, and so they burrow upwards to make shafts: it is these upward tunnels that produce the mole-hills. Later, the young mole can do his digging down to 4ft below ground level.

Moles are really man's friend because they eat wireworms and larvae of other pests and they do help with the draining of the soil. They are, of course, happy in the garden of a composting organic gardener, for worms will there abound to their delight. Basically they are benefactors though we may not like them in our lawns. The best way to keep him at a distance is to plant caper spurge. We have been studying the interesting and fascinating way that this plant, *euphorbia lathyrus*, keeps the mole away. First of all, it seems that the plant cannot do this until its second year—or about that time. It is therefore—I find—advisable to allow the plants to seed themselves. This they will do regularly and generously. The seedlings that arise can be thinned out in the early summer and can be given away or sold to those who need them. Some seedlings must be retained around the parent plant because this will die and the seedling will carry on the good work for another two years. Thus the keeping-away of moles goes on.

What is the power of the caper spurge? Nobody knows! Do the roots give off a scent? Do they emit a kind of radiation wave? Anyway, as far as I can estimate and measure, the distance over which they are effective is 60 yards—almost to an inch.

Onion fly, see *carrot fly*

Peach-leaf curl

The leaves of the peach tree turn red and pucker in the spring and early summer. The result may be defoliation and probably little or no fruit. The answer is to plant garlic around the main trunk of the tree and 2–3ft away; a ring of garlic bulbs may be planted 9in apart. Do not expect results until the spring after planting. Normally plant in April, but it can be delayed until June.

Potato blight

A very common trouble. Irregular blotches appear in the leaves, which soon turn brown or black and are covered with a delicate white mould. The disease spreads faster in muggy weather. In bad cases the disease spores drop to the ground and affect the tubers. Spray with Bordeaux mixture at the end of June and give further sprayings at 3-week intervals. Cut down the haulm and compost it properly, even before harvesting the potatoes. There are varieties of potatoes which are somewhat resistant to this disease. Above all be sure to use disease-free seed potatoes.

Potato common scab

This disease causes the familiar brown, corky scabs to appear on the tubers, in consequence of which the potatoes have to be peeled more deeply, with a lot of waste. The disease is usually more prevalent in districts where the soil is gravelly or sandy, or where it is very alkaline—owing maybe to large applications of lime, or even to the addition of ashes or unbalanced fertilisers. When planting, the trench should be filled up with good powdery compost. Putting a handful of lawn mowings around each potato when planting is helpful.

Sweetcorn cropped in between irises (*Pat Thomas*)

Potato eelworm

Making certain that there is plenty of organic matter in the soil helps to ensure the presence of fungi which actually eat the eelworms. There are resistant varieties of potatoes, particularly worth growing in areas where eelworm is at its worst. With these varieties, even if eelworms do attack there is still a fair crop.

Again, I always put fresh lawn mowings around the tubers in the drills at planting time and this not only prevents the silver scab disease, but delays the tactics of the eelworm as well.

Scab on apples

It is most important to encourage the worms in an orchard. The trees should undoubtedly be growing in a grass sward kept cut regularly, say at least every 10 days. When the leaves fall the worms will pull them into the ground and thus the scab pores will be buried. If a tar-oil wash is used the worms will be killed, and then the leaves must be carefully raked up and composted. Scab can be controlled by spraying with lime-sulphur just before the blossoms open and just after the blossoms have fallen—formula 1 in 30 in the first place, and 1 in 60 in the second. There are varieties which don't like the sulphur, and Bordeaux can then be used instead.

Slugs

If all the beds of roses, herbaceous plants, carnations, cucumbers, lettuce and cabbages, etc, are covered with brown powdery compost or peat humus, 1in deep, then slugs cannot move about and attack the plants.

Window-box pests

Aside from some of the other pests mentioned in this section, the worst pests are sucking insects such as mealybugs and whitefly. This general class of pest will be found on the underside of leaves or in the joints of the plant. When you notice the infestation speedy action is required to prevent its spread to other plants in your house. It is best to quarantine the plant while you treat it with a systemic poison or, even better, while you wash off the colonies of flies or kill the mealybugs with a swab dipped in denatured alcohol. Observe your other plants carefully for these pests spread very easily. If one of the Tagetes family is growing nearby it will often keep away the whitefly.

Winter-moth caterpillars (Tent caterpillars)

The grease-banding of fruit trees was always an annual task years ago, to stop the damage done by caterpillars of the Winter-moth family. The grease traps the climbing wingless female moths when egg-laying. Use a harmless vegetable grease, which can be applied directly to the trunks. Bridges may be formed by leaves, so pick off any that stick to the bands.

Because the females are wingless they remain confined to a small area. There is often no trouble for several years and then the damage may suddenly become serious. The sticky material must be placed in position by late September, and it must be kept clear of leaves and freshened up in the spring. It will then give all the control that gardeners need. On short-stemmed trees grease the lower branches as well as the main stem. The sticky bands should be at least 3in wide.

Woolly aphis

A white, fluffy, cottonwool-like substance is found on apples and it conceals colonies of young aphides. This species may be the means of introducing the disease called canker. The moment you see the cottonwool, paint the affected part with neat liquid derris or rotenone.

13

COMPOST GARDENING IS IMPOSSIBLE

ONE of the problems of being a pioneer in the cult of natural gardening is that there are always those who 'laugh us to scorn' or who put problems which they claim just have not got any answer. Remember that the teaching of this book is never to invert the soil. Always leave it as nature intended it to be, that is with a vertical up and down structure, as though pillars were holding up the surface layer of living soil in which the living organisms can breathe, live (with a capital L) and have their being. It is in this 6in layer or so of living humus-filled soil that the bulk of the feeding roots of plants will develop.

In the vegetable garden, for instance, it is possible to have huge savoys and drumhead winter cabbage, delicious to eat, succulent and healthy, but with all their roots congregated in the 6–7in top layer of living soil. They will be standing up straight and will not topple over. They will not attract the cabbage butterflies so that neighbours can have caterpillars galore eating their brassicas, while the compost-gardengreens are perfectly free.

—Impossible with sprouts

I have as an author, writer and lecturer been accused of going back on my word: in my early books I said that deep digging was absolutely necessary for brussels sprouts, for instance, and now I grow far better sprouts—as do many other gardeners—with no digging at all. Well, I truly believed what I taught—it was what I practised: gardening myself and writing about what I did. But I was converted to compost growing in 1939–40, because of the teaching of Sir Albert Howard, and tried out his methods for myself over the years, so that by 1950 I was able to buy Priors Hall, Thaxted in Essex, with its 13 acres, in order to satisfy myself that organic methods were right, and in fact that they were better. Brussels sprouts, grown the compost way, do *not* need deep digging!

—Impossible with iris

There were those who said you will never be able to grow irises on the compost-mulching method. The rhizomes (the thick root-like part) must lie on the top of the soil and be baked by the sun. What, said my critics, will you do to them? Of course the answer is to plant the irises in the undug soil, leaving the rhizomes on the surface and seeing that the roots below them are firm in the soil. You have to use a trowel to disturb the soil for this purpose. Then after the planting of the whole iris bed is done the powdery brown compost (or peat humus) is put all over the bed an inch deep. Next, with a soft broom brush over the rhizomes, removing the compost and exposing them. The brushing can be done as planting proceeds, if preferred. We have grown beautiful irises in this way for fifteen years—and with no weeds either.

—Impossible with carnations and pinks

Carnations and pinks want lots of lime, the sceptics have told me, so will not grow in an acidy soil, ie a soil with a pH of, say, 4 or 5. The secret of growing these lime-loving plants in a soil tending to acidity is first of all to put a little lime in the hole at planting time, then after planting to sprinkle hydrated lime around them at, say, an eggcupful per specimen. Then, of course, the compost can go into position 1in deep, be it home made or peat humus. Now a year later, when the carnation or pink has grown larger, scoop away the powdery mulch with your left hand at the back or front of the plant and with your right hand pop in a teaspoonful of hydrated lime. Then with the left hand put back the compost and all is well.

Someone will say, 'Take all that trouble to grow border carnations? No thank you!' But the answer to that kind of remark is twofold: either don't bother to grow carnations if your soil isn't suitable, or remember that to grow them the compost way saves *any* hoeing—there will be no weeds, and further, the plants will flower well and the scent will be delicious.

—Impossible in certain soils

The biggest misstatement of them all is that the compost system doesn't suit all soils. The compost mulching certainly suits the sandy soils because they lack humus and, as repeatedly explained, the compost will help to build this up. Furthermore, the mulch on the surface of a dry soil helps to keep what moisture there is in the ground. Sandy soils revel in compost and it transforms them. The worms start to breed as a result and the light-coloured earth gets browner and browner.

Compost on the top of heavy soil makes all the difference also. There is no heavy digging to do—no leaving the soil lumpy and rough in the winter for the frost to act on. The layer of compost on the top causes the worms to come up to pull the organic matter into the clay, and as they do so they make those perpendicular tunnels down which the air can go. They do the digging, in fact, they produce the soil pillars on which the surface soil rests. They clean the soil, making thousands of worm casts, and this not only alters the texture of the soil but, in addition, the plant foods can be increased twenty-fold.

So the compost system works on any soil I have met—in North America, Zambia, Uganda, Australia, South Africa, the Bahamas, France, Cyprus and so on. The system works anywhere, and the interesting thing is that again and again people have told me that there are no worms in their garden, they find they have worms galore within a year of adopting compost growing. Probably there are worm capsules in all soils which have been lying dormant for years and years and which hatch out when the compost is applied. (This was particularly striking in Australia.) Once the worms have hatched they can produce 600 progeny in a year and so the worm population quickly builds up and the good work is done.

OTHER QUESTIONS PEOPLE ASK

If the compost or peat humus keeps down weeds, why doesn't it prevent bulbs and plants growing?

The mulching with compost only controls the annual weeds like pigweed, chickweed, purslane, annual meadow grass and the like. Millions of their seeds lie in the top 2 or 3in of soil, and under the layer of compost they simply do not germinate. Have no annual weeds and you will have daily peace. The bulbs push up through the compost—as do the herbaceous perennials; in fact, they are happy in it and do better.

What about the weed seeds that blow over from my neighbour's garden?

It is surprising how few seeds do blow over in this way. I used to think that the blowing could be serious, but experience over the last fifteen years has proved that very few weed seeds come from 'next door'. Anyway, if they do drop on to the compost it is an easy matter to tweak them out when they are an inch or so high. As they are growing in compost they come up without any difficulty.

Why must the top dressing be compost—why can't sawdust, for instance, be applied?

If what I term 'undigested' organic matter is used as a top dressing, there is invariably trouble. The worms pull some into the soil and the soil bacteria have to get to work on it to compost it and eventually turn it into humus. In doing this they rob the soil of plant foods, particularly nitrogen, and thus what is called denitrification sets in, and plants suffer in consequence. Fallen leaves can be used—but they may contain diseases and weed seeds. It is far better therefore to compost them first. The heat in the compost heap will kill the weed seeds. Further, fresh-fallen leaves may also cause denitrification.

I did put on peat but the birds took it!

Birds will take coarse rough peat moss to make their nests, so always use peat humus. They may even be interested in this the first few weeks and will come and stir it about, but after a short time they leave it alone.

Why do the lawn mowings go 'sludgy' when put on the heap?

Lawn mowings pack down tightly on the compost heap and thus no air can get in between them. So the bacteria that work in airless places get to work and cause putrefaction. Mowings should be put on the heap in 1in layers only, with a thin layer of newspaper over the top of each layer. The paper will prevent the mowings from settling down solid, so that the aerobic bacteria will be able to work properly and there will be no sludge or smell.

Can you put this—or this—on the compost heap?

At every lecture I give, someone in the audience invariably says 'Can you put so-and-so on the compost heap?' I always have to answer 'Everything that has lived can live again in another plant'. The substances that people have suggested cannot go on the compost heap have included sycamore leaves, rhubarb leaves, laurel leaves, yew leaves, nettles, fish bones, cotton shirts, flock from mattresses and even the diseased tops of potatoes.

If the compost is made properly, the temperature engendered in the heap will be 180° F, and this will kill the diseases, the pests and the weed seeds.

Do you put compost on the ground every year?

'It must be expensive putting the compost on the beds every year, isn't it?' This I am asked again and again. You don't put the compost on the beds every year. You put it on 1in deep once and for all. It is only when the worms pull in some of the compost to produce humus down below that more has to be added, just to make up for what has been pulled in. You can easily tell, because the soil may start to show through in patches where the worms have been busy. I have, however, beds which have not had to be topped up with compost over eight years.

Does it matter if you use compost or peat humus? Can you mix them?

It doesn't matter at all from the point of view of improving the soil texture; I use one or the other. And you certainly can mix them. When I have to use peat humus alone, some seaweed manure or fish manure is usually added, at 3oz to the square yard, to give it more nutritive value.

When growing strawberries do you put straw down on the compost?

No—you don't have to use any straw. The compost or peat humus keeps the berries clean—and incidentally prevents the slugs from attacking the plants, because slugs can't move on the powdery compost; they can't get any food and therefore die.

Potatoes—surely you have to dig for these, and earth up, too?

No, all you do is to make a little depression in the rototilled land where the compost has been incorporated and then cover with compost 2in deep. As the plants grow more compost is added. Well-sprouted tubers of early varieties planted in April will usually be up in a week and will be ready for harvesting in eight weeks or so. The harvesting is easy, as the compost can be scratched away from the side and the potatoes used as needed. The compost can then be put back into place. So gradually week by week the potatoes are used as they develop on the roots—until the end of the season.

Can I make my compost in a pit?

Certainly you can—but if the weather is bad your pit will get full of water and the bacteria in the heap will be killed. Thus a sodden uncomposted mass will be produced. Further, it is all very well throwing the vegetable waste into the pit, but at the end of six months when composting time is over, it all has to be dug out and thrown up on the ground above; and this, believe me, is an awful sweat.

Lettuce 'Hilde' on composted ground

My compost heap smells and my neighbour has complained

If the layers of waste are put on evenly, and if at every 6in level a correct organic activator is given, there will be no smell at all. Make certain that the compost bin has air spaces in it so that the 'good bacteria' can breathe.

I am told rats live in compost heaps

The heat engendered in the heap by living bacteria is as high as 180° F, and no rat can live in this! So, compost properly and there cannot be *any* rats.

At Arkley Manor Gardens, visitors say:

'Will you give me £5 for every weed I can find?'

No—I won't because you may find one, but you can easily tweak it out of the compost.

'I never saw raspberry canes 9ft high before.'

I didn't either; at the Swanley Horticultural College we used to reckon on 2 tons of fruit to the acre, and now we can get 9 and 10 tons to the acre.

'Rhubarb—you haven't really got 40 different varieties? Rhubarb is rhubarb, surely?'

There is green rhubarb, tall rhubarb, crimson rhubarb, sweet rhubarb, sown rhubarb, early rhubarb, late rhubarb, and so I could go on. That is why we have published a rhubarb variety leaflet—we tasted all of them, raw and cooked. They are all grown the compost way.

'All the different pot plants grown in the same compost—surely not!'

Yes, we have a very big collection of differing pot plants which people come for miles to see, and one compost does for all of them.

'I never saw four differing crops growing so perfectly together in a frame and so early too.'

Crops that love one another invariably do better when growing in fairly close proximity. So in one frame we have lettuce, radish, cauliflower and tomatoes, and in another broad beans, spinach, early carrots and sweet corn.

'It's fantastic to realise that since you made holes and planted the flowering shrubs, no further cultivations have been done.'

It's extraordinary, but after all it is the whole point of the no-digging, composting scheme. The shrubs grow far better, flower far better, and keep more healthy because of the 1in compost layer on the soil, and because no hoeing is done to disturb the fibrous surface roots.

'Nice raised beds—raised with peat blocks too, all filled with compost; so easy for old people to work.'

Yes, older people love raised beds, and they are easy to make. Ours are 4ft high and 4ft across and are filled with compost.

'I never saw standard gooseberries and standard red currants before.'

They are very useful for those who cannot bend low to do the picking, and crop heavily when mulched with compost or peat humus. The bushes grow on stems 5ft high.

'Your soil must be marvellous because all the differing plants grow so well—and the beautiful brown colour of the soil gives such a glorious background to the flowers and fruits.'

INDEX